C000231561

Dedication

For my Sandra

– always true, always you

CSI
CRIME SCENE IRELAND

KEN FOY is the crime correspondent with the *Evening Herald* newspaper.

He has previously worked for the *Irish Daily Star Sunday*, *Irish Mail on Sunday* and *Wexford Echo* newspapers.

A working journalist since 2000 and a crime correspondent since 2006, Foy was educated at UCD and Griffith College Ireland.

ACKNOWLEDGEMENTS

This book is dedicated to Det Sgt Tom McGrath – a true gentleman, a proper policeman, a brilliant family man and someone who made a massive impression on everyone who ever met him with his gentle kindness, innate decency and sharp sense of humour.

I would like to express my deep gratitude to my wife Sandra – who has always been there for me with her boundless love and support.

This book, like articles written by crime correspondents every day in our newspapers would not be possible without the help of gardai - who despite the most draconian sanctions for talking to journalists that exist in any modern democracy – risk their careers so the public can get some idea of what is going on. And for this I express my sincere gratitude to all of you who I can't name here.

I must also acknowledge the unwavering and simply incredible back-up that my parents have always provided for me.

The help that I have got from my friends in journalism is something that is very much appreciated – in particular these include Niall O'Connor and Charlie Mallon of The Evening Herald, Ali Bracken of the Irish Daily Mail, Niall Donald and Mick McCaffrey of the Sunday World, Alison O'Reilly of the Irish Mail on Sunday and Cathal McMahon of the Irish Daily Mirror.

A special mention must be made here to two of the best newspaper editors in the country – Des Gibson of the Irish Daily Star who gave me my big break and always believed in me and Stephen Rae, the recently appointed Irish Independent editor whose sound advice and knowledge of crime in Ireland is something that I have been lucky enough to benefit from.

Ken Foy,
September, 2012.

Paperweight

First published in 2012 by Paperweight Publications, Level 4, Building 5,
Dundrum Townhouse Centre, Dublin 16, Ireland.

9781908813091
CSI - Crime Scene Ireland

Printed and bound in the UK by
CPI Group (UK) Ltd, Crodon, CR0 4YY

Paperweight Publishing Group, Level 4, Building 5,
Dundrum Townhouse Centre, Dublin 16, Ireland.

www.paperweightpublications.ie

CONTENTS

INTRODUCTION

CRIME SCENE IRELAND is the story of some of the most high profile and successful garda investigations in recent times.

Evidence collected at crime scenes has always been of central importance to criminal enquiries but with rapid technological advances, this kind of evidence is becoming more crucial.

These include the use of advanced DNA techniques, the ever growing reliance on mobile phone records, the prevalence of CCTV camera, extreme developments in the process of gathering evidence from tiny fabrics on clothes and continued improvements in the medical field of pathology.

In the 13 crimes that are featured in this book, we explore how talented investigators cracked these fascinating and disturbing cases.

The nature of major investigations has changed dramatically over the last decade or so with huge advances in forensic technology meaning that gardai have many more tools at their disposal.

In this book we explore how gardai cracked the Joe O'Reilly murder case using internet, mobile phone and CCTV technology.

In the Wayne O'Donoghue manslaughter case, gardai were helped by a little known process called triangulation to locate the body of Wayne's victim, young schoolboy Robert Holohan.

And apart from tiny spots of blood and the discovery of miniscule clothes fibres, it was good old fashioned police work that helped nail the killers of Limerick gangland figure Kieran Keane.

CCTV cameras played a huge role in the murder conviction of multiple rapist Gerald Barry who murdered Swiss teenager Manuela Riedo in Galway.

But DNA and cutting edge mobile phone technology were also crucial in getting the violent monster off our streets.

In the case of murdered mum Siobhan Kearney, gardai had to rely on good old fashioned detective work to build a case against her husband Brian.

Brian Kearney might well be a free man today if an eagle eyed detective had not noticed very quickly that her death was not suicide.

The most advanced of forensic evidence as well as mobile phone tracking helped to convict notorious Dublin gangland killers Keith Wilson, Craig White and Michael Taylor Jnr, in three separate feud related murder cases.

In each instance their victims were savagely shot dead.

In the well known case of Catherine Nevin, a fingerprint trawl along with astute and careful observations by senior officers led them to start a case against the so called Black Widow.

Forensics also played an important part in the convictions of the Scissor Sisters Charlotte and Linda Mulhall, who along with Nevin are surely Ireland's most infamous women prisoners.

Vera McGrath and Colin Pinder would never have been convicted in relation to the death of Vera's husband Brian McGrath except that key advances in DNA meant his body could be finally identified over 20 years after his brutal death.

And if feared rapist Larry Murphy had not admitted his crime and tried to fight the case, gardai had all the forensic evidence to prove that he was involved in the crime.

Mobile phone and CCTV evidence played a crucial role in the conviction of wife killer Eamonn Lillis as it proved that he had lied about the events of the morning that Celine Cawley was beaten to death.

This is CSI... by Ireland's greatest gardai.

CSI
CRIME SCENE IRELAND

CHAPTER 1

The Beast Of Baltinglass

When Ireland's most notorious sex offender and first suspected serial killer was released from prison in August, 2010, it created a frenzy among the media and general public.

At around 10am on August 13, 2010, Murphy walked out of Arbour Hill Prison after serving 10-and-a-half years of a 15-year jail term for rape and attempted murder — he was released under an established practice in this country that allows every prisoner to be granted remission equivalent to a quarter of the sentence imposed.

Perhaps never in the history of the State did the release of a criminal from jail attract such publicity.

Dozens of reporters were tasked with tracking, and subsequently trying to find, Murphy in operations that cost media organisations tens of thousands of euro in just a few days.

The public who had seen and read the almost blanket coverage of Murphy in the weeks before his release were whipped into a state of hysteria and in the weeks after his release there were literally hundreds of alleged sightings of Murphy around Ireland.

Several dedicated websites were set up to track the so-called 'Beast of Baltinglass'.

What was happening was unprecedented as the release

generated protests, including a heated meeting near his home village, and the gathering of a 200-strong crowd in Coolock, who wrongly believed he was inside a half-way house for released prisoners.

Apart from the sick crime he had been convicted of, Murphy was — in popular consciousness at least — a suspect in the disappearance of some six young women between 1993 and 1998, mysteries that still grip Ireland and which have never been solved.

A Garda 'cold-case' investigation called Operation Trace reviewed the disappearances of the women: Fiona Sinnott, Deirdre Jacob, Jo Jo Dullard, Ciara Breen, Annie McCarrick and Fiona Pender.

Murphy was interviewed in prison about at least three of these cases by detectives, refusing to co-operate, but ultimately gardai found no specific evidence linking him to the cases.

Tellingly, the disappearances stopped when he was arrested in 2000 and there is little doubt that many senior officers believe he is the man responsible for the murders of some of these women.

Evidence of this could be seen in January, 2012, when specialist gardai took part in a high profile search of an isolated area in Co Wicklow where 12 years before he was caught holding captive a woman he had just raped.

Gardai decided to search the countryside and a hunting lodge in Kilranelagh based on a report compiled by a UK scientist with an interest in studying criminal behaviour.

At this stage it seems highly improbable that Murphy will ever be prosecuted in connection with those missing women as there is no hard evidence linking him to the crimes.

So why is he one of the most feared and hated criminals in our history?

The only crimes that Murphy has ever been convicted of happened on the night of February 11, 2000.

At around 8.15pm on that Friday evening in Carlow town, Murphy abducted the then 26-year-old businesswoman after she opened the door to her car in a secluded carpark.

He demanded her bag, containing the day's takings of IR£700, but then hit out, fracturing the woman's nose.

Dazed and shocked, his victim fell backwards into the car.

Murphy, then aged 36, ordered the stunned woman to move to the passenger seat and remove her bra. He tied her hands and ordered her to take off her shoes before gagging her with a headband.

Murphy then drove the woman's car across a narrow roadway, took her out, and walked her to his own car, putting her in the boot.

The callous rapist then got into the car and calmly turned up his stereo to mask the sound of the woman's efforts to summon help by banging on the inside of the boot.

A keen hunter, Murphy had detailed knowledge of the Wicklow-Kildare-Carlow area.

He drove his victim eight miles from Carlow to a secluded spot called Beaconstown where he stopped his car and pulled her from the boot.

He dragged her to the passenger seat and undressed both himself and the woman. Then he viciously raped her before pretending he was going to take her home.

Murphy revealed during the ordeal that he was married and told his victim the names of his two young children.

After dressing her again, he tied her up with her bra, gagged her once more, and led her back to the boot of his car.

He then headed up into the foothills of the Wicklow mountains and onto an isolated forest track. Once there, he led the woman from the boot again. This time he lay her across the front seats of his car and raped her three times.

When he was finished he tied her hands behind her back and again led her back to the boot of the vehicle.

This time the woman managed to free her hands and attempted to spray Murphy with an aerosol can.

But the canister did not work and Murphy overpowered her and placed a plastic bag over her head.

The woman struggled and Murphy pulled the plastic tightly over her mouth.

The terrified rape victim managed to climb out of the boot but found herself slipping in and out of consciousness.

She was saved from certain death only when two men who were out foxhunting drove up and stumbled upon the nightmare scene.

Murphy sped away and his panic-stricken victim ran to a ditch.

The two men then took her to a Garda station and identified her attacker, whom they recognised from a previous incident in a local pub.

Meanwhile Murphy went home, got into bed without washing himself, and made love to his heavily pregnant wife who was expecting their third child.

It would be Murphy's last night as a free man for over a decade but who knows what would have happened if Ken Jones and Trevor Moody were not out hunting that night.

Mr Jones and Mr Moody came across a car at around 10.15pm, with its sidelights on, parked in their path in a narrow lane between the pine forest on one side and a line of ash trees on the other. They saw a movement at the back of the car.

At first they were not sure what was happening. It was not unusual for courting couples to use the spot. However, they quickly realised they were looking at a man grappling with a pair of human legs kicking out from the boot of his car.

When Murphy saw them he stopped struggling with his victim, jumped back into his car, revved his engine, and drove by them, his car scraping past theirs as he headed towards the main road to Baltinglass.

Mr Jones and Mr Moody recognised the car and the driver.

They then saw a woman in a state of panic running from the lane into the rusted barbed wire strung between the ash trees. She was clearly injured and in a desperate state.

As the two men helped untangle her from the fence, the woman's panic initially increased but they were able to convince her she was saved. They gave her a jacket and drove her to Baltinglass Garda station.

The following day, the men gave statements to Garda Liam Horgan and Sergeant Jack Kelleher, but then, gardai had already built a strong case against Larry Murphy.

Mr Jones explained: "When I got to less than 15 yards from the car, a man came out from behind the car and opened the driver's door and sat in — at this stage I said to Trevor, 'I know this guy, do you?'

"Trevor replied, 'Yes I do'. I focused on his face and I am absolutely sure that I knew this man to be a Murphy chap originally from Randalstown, Stratford on Slaney. I know this man a long time."

Trevor Moody also knew Larry Murphy, explaining to gardai that he first got to know him "when he made a grab at a sister of a friend of mine" in a pub in Donard, Co Wicklow.

"A row broke out and he got a few thumps," Mr Moody added.

Both men gave horrific accounts of the state that they found Murphy's victim in.

"As soon as this man drove away I saw a girl running away from the car towards the ditch. We both got out and went over to the girl. She was all knotted up in the barbed wire.

"She was hysterical, she asked me, 'Are you with him'.

"I said, 'No'. I told her he was gone. Ken, my friend, shouted that he was getting a torch and she asked was he with him and I replied, 'No'."

The men lifted the victim clear from the wire and reassured the traumatised woman who was in a "terrible state, very traumatised".

Mr Jones later recalled: "She had all blood on her face and her hands were tied. She sat into the jeep and she said, 'Only for you, he was going to kill me'. She said 'he had a bag over my head, a plastic bag'."

Mr Jones was later able to point out this bag to investigating gardai who used it as part of their detailed investigation.

The victim was brought to Baltinglass Garda Station by the two hero hunters who had surely saved her life.

Baltinglass was a sleepy west Wicklow backwater town in the year 2000 with a population barely above 1,000 people.

The town's Garda station was not used to dealing with serious crime but all that was to change dramatically when the two farmers and Murphy's terrified victim arrived in the station at 10.35pm.

Inside the station were Garda Peter Cassin and Garda Seamus Murphy, and if they were expecting a typically quiet night, they would be very much mistaken.

In his official statement, Garda Murphy recalled that the trio entered the station and the victim "was very upset and was bleeding from the mouth and nose, in fact her whole face seemed to be covered in blood".

He said: "She had a bra tied tightly around her neck, she was wearing a white top with a light blue cardigan, black trousers and socks. She was not wearing footwear."

The victim was brought to an interview room by Garda Cassin while Garda Liam Horgan arrived back to the station where he and Garda Murphy had a conversation with Mr Jones and Mr Moody about how they met the victim.

Once the gravity of the situation was established, senior officers were immediately contacted — these included then Inspector Patrick Mangan, who later became a Superintendent, Carlow-based Detective Sergeant Jim Ryan, Tullow-based Sergeant Jack Kelleher and Superintendent Michael Hurley.

Later, senior detectives Dominic Hayes, Gerry McGrath and Mark Carroll were drafted in for their expertise in dealing with serious crime.

Hayes and McGrath are still serving detectives – among the most respected in the force. It would be this nucleus of around a dozen officers that would crack the Larry Murphy case.

Garda Peter Cassin was the member in charge at Baltinglass Garda Station that night.

While his colleague talked to the two men who had saved the victim's life, Garda Cassin used all his skill to reassure the victim who was "during all of this time trembling and crying".

He put his arm around her as she cried and continued to shake.

The victim showed him her knee, which was badly skinned, and she later informed him that she had been taken from Carlow and raped.

Garda Cassin organised for her sister to come to the station.

In his statement, Garda Cassin said: "At this point she broke down crying and shivering."

The garda — who went on to become a well-respected detective based in Rosslare Harbour — held the victim's hand and again "reassured her that she was safe now and no-one was going to hurt her".

As they waited for the victim's sister, she gave her first account to gardai of what happened on that terrible night while she drank a cup of sweet tea.

Crucially, the victim revealed that "the man spoke about the fact that he had two kids" and Murphy had named these children.

After the victim's sister arrived in the interview room, she complained about the bra that was still tied tightly around her neck.

Garda Cassin gave her sister a knife to cut it away and the bra was then put in an evidence bag.

At 12.45am on February 12, the victim was brought from Baltinglass Station to Dublin's Rotunda Hospital, accompanied by her sister and three gardai in an unmarked patrol car.

In the Rotunda, she had a detailed medical examination in relation to the sexual injuries she received before being transferred to the Mater Hospital for X-rays and treatment to her severe facial injuries, which included a broken nose.

Later that night, Garda Liam Horgan travelled with the two hunters to the remote spot at Kilranelagh Lower where Murphy had been caught.

Garda Horgan found the plastic bag that Murphy had used in an attempt to smother the victim.

He preserved the scene and stayed there until 6.30am when he was relieved by Garda Cassin.

At 9.30am, specialist crime scene officers arrived at the scene and a full technical examination took place there.

Earlier that morning, the victim had been brought back to Baltinglass Garda Station where she again outlined her horrific ordeal and gave a full statement to Garda Aoife Casey.

An abridged outline of the statement she gave that morning — condensed to protect the victim's identity — reads: "I first noticed him standing opposite my car. He looked distracted and was pacing back and forth.

"He started towards me and came around the back of the car. It startled me. He said something like, 'Give me the money'.

"He hit me in the face as I tried to get into the car. I struggled and he put his two hands on my neck and forced me over to the passenger seat.

"He got the keys off me and held my head down over the handbrake with his elbow. I couldn't free myself from his grip.

"He moved the car a short distance and at that stage I thought he would just rob me and then drive somewhere to let me go.

"Then he tied my hands with my bra, which he had forced me to take off. My hands were tied really tightly.

"He asked me to give him the money again. I felt numb with shock and fear. I thought he was going to kill me there.

"By now he had covered my mouth with a headband. He told me to take off my boots.

"I couldn't because my hands were tied but he took them off.

"He got out of the car and pulled me out. I thought he was going to leave me there.

"There was another car there. I was kicking and screaming.

"He made me walk in front of him with his hand on my back.

"The next thing I knew the boot of the other car was open — he caught me by the back of the neck and pushed me in head first with a lot of force.

"I kept kicking and screaming. When he put me into the boot I was facing outwards.

"I could feel small flat metal things under me. There was a smell of oil and a football. I could feel something behind my head.

"Then he started driving the car and playing music really loud. We seemed to be going very fast."

After about 25 minutes Murphy stopped the car in an area called Eatonstown, about five miles from Carlow town.

The victim continued: "I could hear the click of the boot. He pulled me out and pushed me in front of him into the driver's seat and told me to sit down. We were in a field, very mucky like a dirt track. I couldn't see any lights.

"The driver's seat was pushed back and I could see a baby chair behind me."

She was than savagely raped as Murphy tried to kiss her on the neck and face. He then forced her to perform oral sex on him.

The brave victim continued: "I felt so numb, I couldn't move. I just hoped it would all end. I feared for my life the whole time, I thought, 'This is it'.

"He asked me if I was married. I lied and said yes.

"He told me he was married and had two boys. My hands were blue — the bra was tied so tightly around my wrists they were really hurting me.

"He loosened the knot and took me out of the car again.

"He told me to put my clothes back on, but I couldn't. He put on my trousers.

"This time he tied my hands behind by back with a headband and tied my bra around my mouth.

"I pleaded with him not to put me in the boot, but he said he had to because I'd start making noise.

"This time we travelled for about 20 minutes. I knew at that stage I was on country roads.

"After having pleaded with him I knew he still wasn't going to bring me home."

After travelling on remote, narrow and dark country roads for 20 minutes, Murphy once again stopped the car.

The victim recalled: "He opened the boot again. I could hear a click.

"We were on a dirt track. It felt like the car was on a slope and I thought he was going to drive into a river. I felt I had no chance.

"He took me from the boot again and sat me in the passenger seat.

"He lay down and said, 'Make love to me'. I said, 'If I do, will you bring me home?'.

"He said he would — I knew deep down he wouldn't. He was

trying to make me feel guilty for him as if he were the innocent one."

Murphy untied the girl and forced her to strip herself and then savagely raped her several times.

At this stage Murphy began to panic and tied the terrified woman up once more.

She told gardai: "He put me into the boot again and closed it. He told me to face inwards."

The victim noticed a brown furniture cleaning spray which was broken – she pressed the top of the aerosol but it would not work.

"He put a white plastic bag over my head and I could smell some chemical. I felt light-headed and couldn't breathe.

"He kept holding the bag over my mouth and I definitely felt like I was going to die.

"I managed to get my right foot over the boot of the car and kept struggling until eventually I had my two legs over and I could feel my legs on the ground and I was slipping down, he still had the bag over my face and the pain was just....

"The next thing I remember I was crawling on the ground and he was gone."

A jeep carrying the two hunters then came by and rescued the woman and brought her to Baltinglass Garda station.

At 8.20am on that Saturday, now-retired Det Sgt Jim Ryan went to the home of Larry Murphy at Woodfield, Baltinglass, with local gardai Liam Horgan, James Lawlor and Michael Curtin.

It was eight hours earlier that Det Sgt Ryan had been informed of the victim's ordeal after he was phoned by gardai from Baltinglass and before he went to Murphy's home, the detective spoke with the victim who had outlined what happened.

In his statement, Det Sgt Ryan recalled going to the property.

"I saw a blue Fiat Punto car, reg no. 97 Ke 3863 at the rear of the house," the statement said.

"I rang the door bell and a man answered the door. I asked him if he was Larry Murphy and he said he was. I introduced myself to him. I told him I was making enquiries into the abduction of a girl from Carlow and the rape of the girl.

"Larry Murphy put his hands up to his head."

At this stage, the detective told Murphy he was being arrested for rape and gave him the standard caution.

Det Sgt Ryan said: "The time of the arrest was 8.25am. Larry Murphy then said, 'I don't know why it happened. I am terrible sorry'.

"I asked him what brought him to Carlow and he said, 'I was doing a house in Bennekerry with my brother Tom — why did I do that?'

"Larry Murphy went to the bedroom and his wife got up and went to the living room. Larry spoke to her there."

In his statement, Garda Liam Horgan recalled that when the officers went into his house with Murphy after his arrest "the suspect nodded his head and turned around and went into the living room/kitchen area of the house".

He said: "The suspect asked if he could tell his wife before we did. Det Sgt Ryan accompanied the suspect down to the hallway to the first bedroom on the left. His wife came out of the room in her pyjamas and she was surprised to see us there.

"Larry Murphy, the suspect, was trying to talk to her. She went into the living room and sat down on the couch. As the suspect walked by her to sit down beside her I heard him say, 'I raped a girl last night'.

"Mrs Murphy was shocked, Det Sgt Ryan tried to explain the circumstances for us being there.

"The suspect asked if he could go to the bathroom to comb his hair. I followed him into the bathroom. As he combed his hair while he looked in the mirror I heard him say, 'Why did I do it?'.

"The suspect returned to the kitchen area, Det Sgt Ryan asked Mrs Murphy the whereabouts of the legally held rifle of the suspect. Mrs Murphy said that it was in a bedroom, the suspect stated, 'No, it's up here', and he pointed to the top of the built-in presses in the utility room and reached up his hand to get it.

"Myself and Det Sgt Ryan reached up and we took down the gun. The suspect stated that it was loaded and while Det Sgt Ryan and myself held the gun, the subject ejected a bullet out of the breach of it.

"I took possession of this rifle and I later handed it over to Garda Lawlor. While the suspect was in the utility room, he stooped down at the window near the back door and said, 'I didn't need to do it.'"

Sgt Jack Kelleher arrived at Murphy's house at 8.30am, having previously taken a statement that morning from Trevor Moody, one of the hunters who had saved the victim's life.

Sgt Kelleher later recalled in a statement: "I met Det Sgt James Ryan and he informed me that he had arrested Larry Murphy for rape. As Larry Murphy was leaving the house he went over to his wife, who was seated, his hands were outstretched and he said to her, 'I'm sorry.'"

As Murphy was brought to Baltinglass Garda Station, Garda Michael Curtin was placed in charge of Murphy's Fiat Punto, which was later transported back to the station for detailed forensic examination.

Meanwhile back in Carlow at the scene of the abduction, gardai recovered the victim's car and some days later a fingerprint was lifted from the car's boot, which matched prints taken from Larry Murphy on that Saturday in Baltinglass Station.

Murphy arrived at the station at 8.50am, where Garda Seamus Murphy was the member in charge. Murphy was read his rights in relation to custody regulations.

In his statement, Garda Murphy later gave a statement that outlined that at 8.54am, Murphy requested a solicitor and declined a breakfast.

Garda Murphy's statement said: "I then asked the prisoner to empty out his pockets, he handed me a large wad of notes saying, 'That's that girls money'. I counted IR£700 in cash."

A short time later Garda Murphy heard Det Sgt Ryan ask Mr Murphy where the girl's handbag was.

The statement said: "Mr Murphy replied, 'It's in the boot of the car'. He then handed me another wad of money stating, 'That's my money'. I counted IR£444.32."

At 1.25pm that Saturday afternoon, Murphy was fingerprinted

and photographed in the station.

At 5.10pm, Murphy provided blood, pubic hair, head hair, saliva and nail scrapings to the investigation team.

But before then, Murphy made admissions to his crime to then Inspector Patrick Mangan and Detective Mark Carroll.

Speaking about the abduction, Murphy said: "I was walking down the path and I seen this girl walking towards me. I had never met the girl in my life. I just flipped. I said to her to give me your money. She said fuck off. I hit her then."

Murphy then tied up his victim and put her in the boot of his car before driving for 20 minutes then stopping the car and raping her and then putting her back in the boot.

He then drove for another 20 to 25 minutes before reaching the remote location near Baltinglass where he took her out of the boot again.

His statement reads: "I put her back sitting in the car. I took the bra off her hands [he had tied her hands with it] I started talking to her. I told her I had two kids. She asked me their names. I told her **** and ***** [names deleted to protect children's identity].

"I asked her had she any kids. She said she hadn't. She said she would like kids. Yeah, I said kids are lovely. She says I will do anything for you, just leave me home. I said I will leave you home. I want to leave you home."

Murphy then raped the terrified victim again and put her back in the boot of his car but in his interview with gardai he brazenly tried to claim that what happened was consensual sex.

He continued: "When I was putting her back in the boot a jeep came and she started to shout. I panicked and just drove off. I did not try to kill her at any stage. I did not try to put a bag over anyone's head last night."

Apologising to the gardai for what he had done, Murphy explained what happened after he fled the scene: "I went to the Stratford Arms pub and I bought a bottle of whiskey. I drank some of it on the way home. When I got home my wife was in the kitchen. The children were in bed.

"The bottle of whiskey is still in the car. I just went to bed. I threw my clothes on the floor. I slept in the nip. This morning the guards called to my home at about 8am to 8.30am. I was dressed in the clothes I wore last night when I went to the door to answer."

Admitting that he was wearing different underwear to what he had worn the night before, Murphy said he had left the underwear on the bedroom floor.

"I was kind of expecting the guards. I didn't sleep much last night," he said before explaining that he told his wife Margaret that he had "raped a girl last night".

Gardai then took Murphy's clothes for forensic testing after his wife dropped down alternative clothing to him in the station. The underwear were also recovered and tested.

Later that day, Murphy was interviewed by senior detectives Dominic Hayes and Gerry McGrath.

During this, he pointed out locations on a map provided by the detectives of the route he had taken and the locations where the crimes took place. He also gave an account of what had happened.

A short time later, Murphy was shown items that had been recovered from his car including the victim's car keys, shoulder bag and black knickers. He also agreed that a pair of blue underpants were his.

At 8pm that Saturday, Murphy was charged in the station with rape and brought before a special sitting of Baltinglass District Court.

With Murphy in custody, the case against him was further strengthened when a woman gave gardai a statement about seeing him in Carlow on the night of the abduction and rape just before he kidnapped his victim.

A woman known to Murphy also came forward a week after the crimes and gave gardai detailed information about an incident in the summer of 1996 when Murphy assaulted her and throttled her throat.

She explained that when she was in a car on her own with him, he drove to an isolated spot in Co Kildare.

She described the terrifying situation to gardai: "Suddenly

without saying anything he put his left arm around my shoulder. I cannot remember exactly, but he may have put his right hand on my leg.

"I was wearing shorts and a T-shirt. I asked what was he doing and pushed him back. Suddenly he grabbed me with both hands around the throat and pushed me down towards the door and the front seat of the car. He said nothing.

"His expression had totally changed on his face and this was a side of him that I had never seen before. I got my hand on the door handle beside me and broke his grip on my neck. I jumped out of the car and he grabbed me again from behind this time by the upper arms."

The assault ended with Murphy expressing concern that the victim did not inform his wife about what had happened. Murphy was never charged for this incident.

On May 11, 2001 — after spending 15 months in custody — Murphy was handed a 15-year sentence, which he served in Arbour Hill Prison, a Dublin jail where the vast majority of offenders are sex offenders.

While serving his sentence Murphy refused to undergo any treatment or counselling and also expressed no remorse for his sickening crime.

As time went on he became more isolated from his family and by the time that he was released he had effectively been disowned by them.

Speaking after his release in August 2010, Murphy's only brother Tom said: "Larry Murphy should be very, very ashamed of himself. He has dragged everybody that was in any way involved with him down to the ground.

"If he had any decency in him he would have at least have stopped at one of the microphones and said sorry to his victim.

"There was never any remorse shown. I don't know how any person could carry out a crime like that and not be prepared to at least say sorry to the victim.

"That woman deserves these words: I am sorry."

However, Tom said that even if his brother said sorry he would still disown him. Tom said: "I will not have Larry back. I don't want him in my life.

"I can't fully speak for my sisters, but they may be talking along the same lines."

He added: "He won't be accepted back into their homes under any circumstances."

Just days after his release Murphy fled Ireland and the next confirmed sighting of him was when a newspaper snapped him drinking and socialising in Amsterdam in late November of 2010.

In May 2011, Murphy returned to Ireland for a number of weeks after his passport was stolen in the Spanish city of Barcelona where he had been living for a few months.

During that time in Ireland, he stayed in a number of hotels and a safe house provided by a group who help former prisoners resettle in the community.

Around a month later, he slipped out of country on the Rosslare to Cherbourg ferry in a disguise. He has not been back since and is believed to be living in continental Europe.

CHAPTER 2

When Evil Comes Knocking

There were 460 suicides in Ireland in 2006 and when the body of Siobhan Kearney was discovered in her home in leafy and affluent south Dublin, it looked like she would be adding to that statistic.

After all, Siobhan (38) had suffered a breakdown in 1999 and had even been looking for tablets for depression the night before she was killed.

The body of the pretty and vibrant mother-of-one was discovered by her dad, Owen McLaughlin.

He had been forced to kick in her locked bedroom door before making the grim discovery at the Goatstown residence on the morning of February 28, 2006.

Earlier, Mr McLaughlin and his wife Deirdre had been called to the house by Siobhan's younger sister Niamh, who had arrived there at 9.30am to find Siobhan's three-year-old son Dan walking around the house on his own in a distressed state.

Mr McLaughlin later described the horror of the situation.

He said: "I shouted Siobhan's name three or four times very loudly and with no response I put my shoulder to the door and ran at it with my shoulder and used my feet and broke the door down."

His daughter's lifeless body was lying in the foetal position on the floor near the en suite bathroom and there was a vacuum cleaner cable around her neck. He put his hand on Siobhan's arm and leg and felt that she was cold. Mr McLaughlin knew his beloved daughter was dead.

The emergency services and Siobhan's husband Brian were immediately called as little Dan cried in the background.

Brian Kearney, whose 49th birthday occurred that day, quickly arrived at the house and the first words he said to Siobhan's mother Deirdre were: "We were going to be together forever."

It was a horrible, confused scene as Siobhan and Kearney's siblings arrived at the house in the plush Knocknashee estate located just a stone's throw from the well-known Goat pub.

Fire brigade and ambulance personnel had been quick to arrive at the house and they suspected Siobhan had taken her own life.

Fire officer Neil Hogan even searched the bedroom for a suicide note or for medication or drugs but did not find anything there.

Just a minute earlier, his colleague Alan Finn had observed that Siobhan was definitely dead. Later, he recalled that he saw "some marks around the neck and some blood pooling along the face".

It did not take long for gardai to arrive at the scene. One of the first officers there was family friend Sergeant Charlie McConalogue, who had been told the devastating news in a phone call from Siobhan's sister Brighid McLaughlin.

Sgt McConalogue had previously been in a relationship with Siobhan before her marriage to Kearney and he had been friends with her for 30 years.

So it must have been especially traumatic for the garda to see her body. Sgt McConalogue later described what he saw when he walked into the bedroom.

He said: "When I looked in the door of the bedroom I could see the body of my late friend Siobhan Kearney. I had known her more commonly as Siobhan McLaughlin for more than 30 years.

"Her feet were facing the window of the bedroom. Her hands and feet were very white. I also noticed her face was very purple in colour.

"I observed scratch marks on her chin and face," he said.

This must have been a terrible experience for the sergeant, but he remained composed in the house that day and some of his observations played a crucial part in leading to the conviction of Brian Kearney for the murder of his wife — two years after he thought he committed the perfect crime.

One of the country's most respected and experienced gardai at that time, Detective Inspector Martin Cummins — who was based in Blackrock Station in south Dublin for many years — arrived at the scene and like most other observers, he initially thought that Siobhan had taken her own life.

Arriving at the house at 11.35am on that crisp February morning, now retired Det Insp Cummins went into the bedroom where he saw Siobhan's body.

Moments later, he decided that her death was much more sinister than suicide.

He said: "The circumstances presented to me that it was possibly a suicide and that some photographs would be helpful for an inquest.

"However, having made certain observations and heard certain things I decided that the situation was a lot more sinister.

"I decided the services of a full Garda technical team would be required and I then evacuated the house and contacted Detective Superintendent Oliver Hanley and Professor Marie Cassidy."

A source close to the investigation told this author that the detective's "quick thinking and expert handling" of the case was crucial to Brian Kearney's prosecution.

"This situation had all the hallmarks of a suicide so making the call he did at such an early stage was crucial," the source said.

"Every crime scene is different and the right call needs to be made and that is exactly what happened that morning."

The source added: "Apart from what he observed at the scene, Detective Inspector Cummins quickly came to the conclusion that Brian's behaviour and reaction to his wife's death was suspicious in the extreme."

Det Insp Cummins, along with Det Sgt Michael Gibbons, led the lengthy investigation and they were greatly helped by Sgt Charlie McConalogue's observations of Brian Kearney's behaviour in the house that morning.

When Sgt McConalogue informed Kearney that detectives wanted to speak to him, he said: "Charlie, Charlie, will I be fit to go through with it?"

Later Kearney asked him about his clothes. Sgt McConalogue recalled: "Brian Kearney asked me, 'Charlie, can I go now?' I said, 'I don't think anyone can leave the house, including myself'. He said, 'Charlie, will the detectives want my clothing?' I said the detectives would have to decide that.

"I was taken aback by it. Before I left the house, I informed the detectives what he had said to me. My understanding was he left the house in the same clothing."

Meanwhile, when questioned by detectives, Kearney admitted that he and his wife had been sleeping in separate bedrooms. All did not seem right with the marriage.

To outside observers, the couple seemed to have it all. He ran a lucrative electrical contract business and they owned a plush hotel in the Mediterranean island of Majorca.

They had loving and loyal families and a beautiful little son. But there were serious cracks in their marriage. Cracks that ultimately led to Siobhan's murder.

Their relationship had never been the most smooth.

They had first dated back in 1989 when she was a 21-year-old chef in a canteen in an electronics factory in Mulhuddart, west Dublin, where he also worked.

They ended up moving into his house in Ballinteer, which he shared with his daughter, Aoife, from another relationship. The couple were briefly engaged but broke up in 1995 after reported differences over a pre-nuptial agreement.

She stayed in touch with him, and they reunited years later. She moved into his new house, Carnroe, in Knocknashee, Goatstown. And when she got pregnant again, after suffering a miscarriage, they got married in January 2002.

Meanwhile, just over 48 months later, on the evening of Siobhan's death, Det Insp Cummins called to Kearney's parents' home to get the clothes that he had been wearing that morning, but Kearney's elderly mother Maeve told gardai she had washed the clothes because they were "sweaty and soiled".

This compounded the deep suspicions that gardai had about Kearney but huge work needed to be done in this case.

Because Kearney lived in the house with Siobhan and there was no sign of a break-in, DNA evidence was never likely to be a huge factor but a thorough forensic examination of the home took place anyway.

Fingerprint expert Detective Christopher O'Connor spent hours gathering fingerprints from the house. He found fingerprints belonging to Siobhan and to Brian Kearney in the bedroom where her body was found.

But crucially, the vacuum cleaner flex found around her body tested negative for fingerprints.

This was going to prove to be a very difficult case to crack and the investigation team had to dig very deep to find a motive for murder.

The investigation focused on a number of different strands, including examining the marriage, the couple's financial situation and disproving the theory that Siobhan had taken her own life.

Gardai spent days forensically examining the house. They even travelled to Majorca, where Kearney and Siobhan were running a six-bedroom boutique hotel in Soller — bought for €2.2 million less than four years before Siobhan was murdered — but they failed to find any significant evidence there.

Routine enquiries by officers established that Kearney and Siobhan's marriage was in deep trouble.

Gardai established that in the weeks before her death, Siobhan had begun to take active steps to formally separate from her husband and had engaged a family law solicitor to act for her.

Detective Paul Johnstone, a computer forensic expert, analysed a laptop recovered from the house in Goatstown and he discovered Siobhan had been searching websites for the Irish Law Society and the subject of 'free legal aid' was accessed from the laptop.

Gardai also discovered that on the night before Siobhan was found dead in her home, she e-mailed her brother's partner in Italy which she ended by asking her to "say a prayer for me".

Siobhan e-mailed her brother Owen's partner Alessandra Benedetti, who speaks Italian and German, to thank her for translating information.

In the e-mail Siobhan said life was hectic with all the excitement of her baby nephew George who was just like a "little marshmallow".

She described her son Dan as "all action I just can't keep up with him he's just mad out, wild, wild, wild, I don't know what I'm going to do, he loves Madonna and wants to listen to her CDs all day and then watch John Wayne movies".

"He's football mad," she wrote. "I've lost three pounds in the last week. I hate the thought of when he's due to go back to school. Say a prayer for me."

In the e-mail she said Ms Benedetti would know what it was like, having sons of her own, and said she was excited about the couple coming to Ireland to visit in April.

She added that she couldn't wait to meet her nephews.

This e-mail left the investigation team in no doubt that Siobhan's frame of mind was far from suicidal just 12 hours before her body was found.

Officers also established that letters sent by her solicitor to Kearney seeking a trial separation went unanswered. When questioned by detectives about this, a week after the murder, Kearney said he felt no animosity about his wife's desperate wishes for a divorce.

He also denied that he killed her. Detective Sergeant Michael Gibbons put it to him that he killed his wife and Kearney replied: "No, no guard, I didn't do it."

When asked by detectives why he killed his wife, he said: "I did not kill Siobhan."

At this stage, gardai were drawing accurate conclusions as to why Kearney killed his wife. They enlisted the services of a forensic accountant called Toni Massey to examine the couple's financial affairs.

She discovered that even though Kearney had a considerable

number of assets and on paper he was worth a substantial amount of money, he was in a difficult position in that he was overstretched on borrowing.

He had received a letter from the bank telling him his borrowings needed to be reduced.

His mortgage repayments at the time were €15,000 when his monthly income was €10,000. Despite owning around €5 million in assets, Kearney was up to his neck in debt.

In the event of a marriage separation, Siobhan wanted to move out of the home she shared with Kearney and into the adjacent house that they owned in the Knocknashee estate.

After examining Kearney's financial affairs, gardai established that he needed to sell the house that she wanted to move into. Crucially, this gave him a motive to kill.

The forensic accountant was not the only technical expert that gardai relied on in this case.

A source close to the investigation told this author that the evidence of Dr Neal Murphy, a qualified mechanical engineer and lecturer in UCD, was crucial to securing a conviction.

He carried out tests on the flex of the Dyson vacuum cleaner that was discovered on Siobhan's body and established that it could not have held her weight for more than five to seven seconds. This proved that it was highly unlikely that she committed suicide by hanging herself.

Instead, gardai believed that Kearney strangled his wife and then attempted to make her death look like suicide by hoisting her body over the door of the bedroom with the vacuum flex.

The reason for this belief was a post-mortem examination carried out by State Pathologist Dr Marie Cassidy, which showed that three breaks in Siobhan's neck were consistent with manual strangulation.

At Kearney's murder trial in February 2008, Dr Cassidy outlined what she thought had happened to Siobhan that terrible morning.

"She was assaulted while in bed, grabbed on the neck, rendered semi-conscious, at which point the ligature (the flex) would have been applied, hastening her death," she said.

Dr Cassidy also explained that Siobhan had some bruises on her lower body which could have been caused in a struggle with an assailant and would have been consistent with ligature strangulation.

She said the time of death was estimated to be first thing in the morning of February 28, 2006, between 6am and noon.

Gardai had spent many months gathering all this technical evidence which showed that Siobhan had not committed suicide and that Kearney had a financial motive to murder his wife.

Within minutes of examining the house at Goatstown, they had concluded that there had not been a break-in there, so if Siobhan had not killed herself and no intruder had entered the house, this meant that gardai had only one suspect — her husband, who admitted being in the house on the morning of the murder and leaving it at 7.37am.

While gardai and Siobhan's family were convinced that she had been murdered by her husband, it was ultimately the DPP who had to make the big decision to press charges in a case that was based on circumstantial evidence.

Such a decision must have seemed light years away on the night of December 10, 2006, when Siobhan's family and friends held a vigil outside the home where she was murdered.

Brain Kearney was absent from the house next door, which he had moved into after the murder, but in what was seen as a provocative gesture he left a wedding picture of the once happy pair in the window of the living room, facing out towards the mourners.

A crowd of 200, many of whom carried candles and pictures of the smiling blonde hotelier, heard Siobhan's sister Aisling McLaughlin make an impassioned plea for her murderer to hand himself in.

"Siobhan didn't choose to die, someone else made that choice for her... they decided Siobhan should die. Will that person please come forward for everyone's sake, and tell the truth," she said.

But investigations and enquiries were ongoing at this stage and matters were at an advanced stage.

Brian Kearney was not charged with her murder until May 30, 2007 — a full 15 months after he committed the brutal crime.

A source close to the investigation explained: "It was a very protracted case. It took a long time to build up a case and it was done strand by strand, block by block.

"There were many meetings with the DPP before the charge was brought and there was some concern that we were relying overwhelmingly on circumstantial evidence.

"But when you note all the different strands in this case, it really becomes very compelling and leaves no doubt that Brian Kearney murdered his wife."

On the morning of May 30, 2007, Kearney was awoken by detectives banging on the front door of his Goatstown home at 6.45am, where he was arrested and brought to Dundrum Garda Station.

After being cautioned by Detective Sergeant Michael Gibbons and then charged, he replied "not guilty".

Less than three hours after his arrest, Kearney was brought to Dun Laoghaire District Court, where he was formally charged and remanded in custody to Cloverhill Prison.

Dressed in a grey jumper, jeans, socks and sandals, Kearney clasped his hands during the short hearing.

Chewing gum, he remained impassive and did not look at the McLaughlin family, who were seated at the back of the small court for the short hearing, where they sobbed and held hands.

A week later, Kearney was granted bail after his brother Patrick put up an independent surety of €55,000.

Kearney pleaded not guilty but he was convicted after a dramatic trial at the Central Criminal Court in the spring of 2008, which lasted for three weeks.

Day after day the stony-faced murderer sat in the court barely ever displaying a flicker of emotion.

The former electrician arrived at court every day with his elderly parents Feargal and Maeve, his sister Laurie and his daughter from a previous relationship, Aoife.

Heartbroken Aoife sobbed and held her killer dad's hand when the jury gave their guilty verdict after five-and-a-half hours of deliberation on March 5, 2008. He did not even flinch when given the news that signalled a life behind bars.

Also in court every day and usually all dressed in black were Siobhan's family — her parents, Owen and Deirdre McLaughlin, and their seven children, Ann Marie, Brighid, Caroline, Niamh, Deirdre, Aisling and Owen.

Just minutes after the verdict was reached, the McLaughlins formed a cordon by linking arms alongside the prison van that reversed up to the Four Courts building to take Kearney away to Mountjoy Prison for the first night of his life sentence.

The McLaughlin family had been convinced of Kearney's guilt from day one.

They knew that Siobhan desperately wanted to leave her husband and just hours after her body was found, her dad Owen had noticed that Kearney was not showing much emotion about his wife's death while Siobhan's sister Brighid noted "very odd" comments made by Kearney.

The relief and sadness of the McLaughlin family was clear for everyone to see as photographers and reporters swarmed around them in the aftermath of the murder verdict.

Outside the court, Siobhan's sister Aisling told the unruly media scrum in a strong, confident voice: "Today, Siobhan has got justice, we have got justice and Siobhan's murderer has got justice, and for that we are most thankful.

"Since that day, Tuesday, February 28, 2006, our lives have been utterly destroyed by this brutal and pointless act of savagery, from which they cannot, nor ever will be the same.

"But Siobhan has been with us every day since that day, she has never moved and she continues to live in each one of us.

"Siobhan needs peace now, to sleep peacefully, knowing that everything that can be done has been done."

But the agony for the McLaughlin family was not over yet.

Just 15 days after being found guilty of murder, Kearney lodged an appeal against his murder conviction.

His appeal hearing was held on July 28, 2009, and his lawyer argued the quality of circumstantial evidence in the case was poor.

An impassive Kearney stood in court to hear the three-judge panel reject his arguments to have his conviction quashed.

Their court verdict was greeted by applause from members of the victim's family and cheers of "yes" and "put him back in his cage".

It was not until October 2009 that the Court of Criminal Appeal explained why they dismissed Kearney's appeal.

In a written judgement, it was stated that "the compelling nature" of the evidence in the case "was such as to exclude every other reasonable possibility" that Kearney murdered his wife.

This court judgement is something that has pleased the dozens of gardai who worked so hard on the case.

A source close to the investigation explained: "The learned judges' comments are an absolute and total vindication of how the investigation and the trial was conducted.

"It also sets down a very important marker for the future in terms of circumstantial evidence in cases like this. If there are enough strong and solid strands of evidence it will lead to convictions."

Kearney was refused a final appeal before the country's highest court — the Supreme Court — in January 2012 when the Court of Criminal Appeal made a ruling after a hearing that was heard in July 2010.

In the latest motion, he sought permission for his case to be decided by the Supreme Court on grounds that it raised an exceptionally important point of law.

The question was whether it is open to trial judges to admit evidence where they are "mindful" of its possible prejudicial effect on an accused.

For example, his lawyers argued that the fact that the jury was told Siobhan Kearney kept a diary could have led to prejudicial speculation against her husband as to its contents.

The three-judge court refused a Supreme Court hearing on the grounds that the point raised was very specific to the circumstances of this case and does not have general application.

Speaking in the aftermath of that decision, Siobhan's mother

Deirdre McLaughlin said: "Today is the first day of the rest of our lives. He is the killer but he has not won.

"I saw warning signs. I saw the temper he had. He had a coldness. He was not a guy you could sit and have a conversation with.

"He was all work, work, work. She was a hard worker too, but she was kind, loving, a beautiful person inside and out.

"She brought him home to meet me after a while and I knew there was something wrong.

"There was an icy coldness in a room when he entered it. He sucked all the warmth and laughter out of a room. I warned Siobhan. But she saw something in him.

"She asked me after that first meeting, 'Mammy, why didn't you shake his hand?' But I couldn't."

While the McLaughlins will never come to terms with the murder, Brian Kearney has been serving his sentence at Wheatfield where he spends a lot of time reading and working in the prison laundry.

Shortly after he went into prison, Kearney put the luxury hotel that he bought with Siobhan on the market for €3.4 million but the asking price was slashed to €2.75m in just four months as Spanish property prices crashed with the recession.

In July 2011 it was taken off the market and is now run by the killer's brother Patrick.

Jail sources say Kearney rarely mixed with any other prisoners in his first years behind bars.

However, in May 2012, it emerged that he struck up an unlikely friendship behind bars with Michael Hogan (50), a gun nut who is serving 10 years for shooting his neighbour in the stomach.

A jail source explained: "They are always with each other — they are the best of mates and seem to really like each other's company.

"The strange thing about it is they both come from very different backgrounds — Kearney was a top businessman from a privileged background while Hogan has a lengthy criminal record dating from when he was only a young man.

"Kearney was never in any trouble with the law until he murdered his wife while Hogan was well-known to officers even before he shot his neighbour back in September 2008.

"There is no doubt that Kearney would have turned his nose up at someone like Hogan before he was locked up."

Hogan's victim Derek Palmer had four feet of his bowel removed after he was thrown into a wall by the nearly point-blank shotgun blast at Corduff Place in Blanchardstown.

When Hogan was jailed for 12 years with two suspended in June 2011, he warned Mr Palmer "I'll see you later" as he was being led away by prison officers.

Apart from the Corduff Place incident, Hogan has two other firearms convictions dating from 1991 and 1985.

As Kearney got more used to his grim surroundings in the west Dublin jail, he became a fully-fledged member of the Red Cross from behind bars, advising other inmates on issues such as smoking and HIV.

Kearney's most regular visitor to prison is his beloved daughter Aoife and, in September 2011, he was said to be deeply upset at missing her wedding to her long-term partner, which took place at the boutique Hotel Salvia in Majorca.

The wedding in Spain was a lavish affair with dozens of guests flying in from Dublin. However, Kearney's only communication with his daughter on her big day was on the telephone from the grim surroundings of Wheatfield Prison.

This was not the first massive occasion in Kearney's life that he missed because of his incarceration.

In July 2010, when his mother Maeve died after a short illness, Kearney did not apply for temporary release on compassionate grounds to attend her funeral — the killer probably realising that such an application would be turned down by the prison authorities as he was just over two years into a life sentence.

It emerged in the autumn of 2011 that Kearney had taken a new interest in politics behind bars and had been actively encouraging other inmates to vote in that year's presidential election.

Jail sources revealed that Kearney was going from cell door to cell door with forms which prisoners filled out to apply to vote in the big election which was held in late October 2011.

That election was of course won by Labour party candidate Michael D Higgins, who caused controversy in March 2012 when the *Evening Herald* revealed that he was due to visit Wheatfield Prison to watch a production of the play, The Happy Prince.

Even though Kearney did not act in the play, the fact that the Irish President was visiting the jail for such a purpose outraged Siobhan's family because the play was produced by another prisoner — Eamonn Lillis — who was serving a sentence for killing his wife.

Her mother Deirdre McLaughlin felt so strongly about the matter that she wrote to the President.

In the letter, dated March 7, 2012, Mrs McLaughlin wrote: "I feel saddened that I have to write this letter.

"I watched you receive the Seal of Office when you became the President of Ireland. With the wealth of experience you have you were the only person for this important position.

"I have read great things about you.

"I also love poetry and the arts. I felt a great kindness towards you, because in my opinion you are a man for all seasons, a man of the people.

"All that changed last week when I was informed you planned to attend a performance in Wheatfield Prison of The Happy Prince by Oscar Wilde.

"I was not very happy reading this as one of the actors in this play has already taken a life.

"The mayhem that is left behind after such an event never goes away. The family are left with no coping skills, their hearts broken because there was no hugs, no 'see you later', they just vanished from the face of this earth.

"Siobhan was our flesh and blood — she is the bones of us and the heart.

"I feel if you had spoken to some of the families who are affected by violent crime you might have been better informed.

"I find it very upsetting that a gentleman who holds the highest office in the country finds it necessary to attend such a performance in Wheatfield Prison as I believe it will indulge a killer.

"There has to be something more useful you can do that day."

Siobhan is buried at Redford Cemetery in Greystones, Co Wicklow, and her tombstone makes no reference to the fact that she was married. Instead it reads 'Siobhan McLaughlin'.

It is a place that the McLaughlin family often visit as they still try to come to terms with their terrible loss.

But perhaps the most tragic victim in this sorry tale is Kearney and Siobhan's little boy Dan, who is growing up effectively an orphan because of the evil actions of his dad.

CHAPTER 3

Deadly Double Cross

Owen Treacy was soaked in his own blood as he lay clinging to life in a hospital bed.

Just three hours earlier he had been stabbed 17 times in the ear, neck and chest, and had witnessed his uncle and close associate — crime godfather Kieran Keane — shot dead.

The same fate would surely have befallen Treacy if the gun the killers used to murder his uncle had not jammed as they tried to end his life too.

It was January 29, 2003, and the bitter feud between vicious criminals in Limerick was building towards one of its biggest confrontations. Earlier that night, 36-year-old drug lord Kieran Keane had been the victim of an amazing double-cross.

He was duped into thinking two of his main criminal rivals — brothers Eddie and Kieran Ryan — had been kidnapped for him by another gang.

Their father Eddie Snr was the first victim of the Limerick feud — a bloodbath that would go on to make global headlines — when he was shot dead in a packed Limerick bar in November, 2000.

Despite never being charged with the murder, it has always been suspected that Kieran Keane was directly involved and he knew that Ryan's sons Eddie and Kieran would never forget that.

It was perhaps for this reason that Kieran Keane was so keen to meet the 'kidnapped' brothers on that January evening — his last.

When he went to check out the situation with his nephew Owen Treacy (35), the pair were bundled into a car and eventually brought to an isolated spot outside Limerick.

When they arrived there, Keane was tortured by being stabbed six times near his left ear and then murdered by a single gunshot to the head while Treacy was left for dead with multiple stab wounds.

Treacy miraculously survived. But before that brutal murder can be fully explored it is crucial to look back on what had happened in the days, weeks and months before Keane's murder.

The shocking events of January 2003 are unsurpassed in the history of gangland crime in Ireland.

In the space of seven crazy days, Eddie Ryan's two sons, Eddie and Kieran, were 'kidnapped' and feared murdered before showing up alive and well.

This happened just hours after their bitter, criminal rival Kieran Keane was murdered as part of an elaborate double-cross by the McCarthy/Dundon gang.

In the months before these events, the McCarthy/Dundon gang had continued to gain prominence as the bitter feud between the Keane/Collopy faction and the Ryan/McCarthy gang continued.

Before January 2003, the McCarthy/Dundons had not yet fully committed to taking sides in the war — but all that was to change.

The city had been in a very tense state since the murder of gangland hardman John Ryan in Limerick's Moose Bar in November 2000 — a situation made much worse when the Dundon brothers Wayne, Dessie and Ger returned to live in Limerick less than a year later.

Another brother cannot be named here for legal reasons.

It did not take the dangerous Dundon brothers long to get involved in serious criminality, and with their extensive criminal contacts in the UK they were able to import heavy-duty weaponry as well as involve themselves in massive wholesale drug dealing.

The Dundons formed a particularly close alliance with their first cousins Anthony 'Noddy' McCarthy, Larry

McCarthy Jnr and James McCarthy to form the then-nucleus of the McCarthy/Dundon gang.

The shocking murder of innocent bouncer Brian Fitzgerald in November, 2002, showed the depths to which this brutal gang was prepared to sink, but even worse was to follow in the years ahead.

Apart from the obvious problems with the McCarthy/Dundons, gardai in the beleaguered city were becoming more and more concerned that a younger generation was being caught up in the deadly warfare.

One of the most prominent of these teenagers was Kieran Keane's out-of-control nephew Liam.

Liam was the son of Kieran's gang boss brother Christy.

Christy had been jailed for 10 years in May, 2002, for drug -dealing and Kieran was primed to take over as head of the family — but his reign was not to last more than seven months.

Liam was just 17 when he was accused of stabbing tragic Eric Leamy to death after a row over a dog in Limerick's Lee Estate in August, 2001.

Just over two years later he made himself a household name when, after being acquitted of killing Leamy, he cocked his fingers in a V-sign while snarling and smirking at court photographers.

In March 2002, Liam Keane was stabbed in the back in a feud-related attack in Limerick city centre.

Keane told gardai that he had been knifed by Eddie Ryan's son, Kieran 'Rashers' Ryan.

The case was heard in January 2003. Ryan was brutally assaulted by a member of the rival Keane/Collopy faction as he walked into the Limerick Circuit Court, forcing the planned trial to be adjourned for three hours.

When the case finally started, Ryan was charged with assault and two counts of being in possession of, and producing, a knife — but Liam Keane claimed he was unable to identify his attacker.

"Kieran Ryan stabbed me in the back," Keane told the court.

When asked if he could identify Ryan, he replied: "No."

Judge Carroll Moran then said he was left with "no alternative" but to direct the jury to find the accused not guilty.

"It is a very sorry state of affairs that this should happen and if this is going to persist we are going to live in a state of social chaos and anarchy," commented Judge Moran.

The judge could have no idea how true his words were to become — within hours of Kieran Ryan's surprise acquittal, a bizarre and unbelievable kidnap plot unfolded.

January 23, 2003, was a cold night as brothers Kieran and Eddie Ryan and their close associate Christopher 'Smokie' Costelloe were walking along Moylish Road in Ballynanty.

According to the account given by Costelloe, who was later convicted of the murder of Kieran Keane, a black van pulled up, two armed men jumped from it and they tried to bundle them into the back.

"I managed to get away up by the side of the van and I ran towards my house," Costelloe later told gardai.

"As I got to the corner they left a shot after me. I could feel the pellets breeze off the jacket."

He recalled that the Ryan brothers were bundled into the back of the van which sped off into the night while he "kept running".

The Keane/Collopy gang were the prime suspects for the abduction of the two brothers, who were then aged 19 and 20.

Gardai were extremely concerned and there were immediate fears that the brothers had been murdered.

As days passed, tensions in Limerick began to reach breaking point.

The army was drafted in to help the hundreds of gardai who were searching for the young men. The search was concentrated on a remote area near Cratloe Woods in Co Clare, about seven miles from Ballynanty where the kidnapping was alleged to have happened.

Four days after the alleged abduction the brothers' mother Mary — whose husband Eddie had been murdered in cold blood less than two years earlier — acknowledged that they must be dead.

In an emotional interview, Mary Ryan addressed the gang that she thought was responsible, saying: "You are evil, the devil is in you. May a widow's curse be on you for the rest of your life.

"They killed my husband and they walked free. Now they've taken my two children. I just want them back."

Tensions between the feuding sides continued to rise and, five days after the brothers went missing, 20 men from opposing factions were involved in a violent brawl outside Limerick Courthouse.

Some of the fighting gangsters were wearing bulletproof vests — clothing that was to become an essential social accessory in the years ahead in the city.

A senior source who witnessed this brawl told this author: "If gardai had not been on the scene within seconds there could well have been fatalities as a result of this mass brawl. It was a very violent incident that involved a lot of pumped-up criminals who had set their sights on causing a lot of damage to each other."

Despite the huge suspicions that surrounded them in the days that the Ryan brothers were missing, the Keane/Collopy gang continued to operate as normal.

One of their associates is suspected of ringing Mary Ryan during that period and taunting her by falsely claiming that her sons' bodies had been buried with their murdered dad Eddie.

As tensions rose, an associate of the Ryans was involved in an AK47 gun attack on a Keane-controlled property in St Mary's Park.

Then, one week after the abduction, completely out of the blue, Kieran and Eddie Ryan walked into Portlaoise Garda Station and told officers: "We're the boys who were abducted."

The boys were taken by gardai from Portlaoise to Limerick where they had a tearful reunion with their mother Mary at the city's Henry Street Garda Station.

A few hours later, Kieran and Eddie enjoyed a wild and boozy party at their home with their mates and some criminal associates. The event was watched by an amazed press pack.

Kieran Ryan told reporters: "I'm just happy to be alive and to see my whole family, especially my baby daughter."

When asked where he had been all week, he said he didn't know because he had been "covered up".

He added: "I got threatened and I'm not going to talk to no-one about it. I've been threatened not to talk."

As Kieran cuddled his four-month-old daughter Kelsey, he said he believed for a week that he was going to be executed.

He added: "From the time I got taken to the time I got home I thought I was going to be dead. I'm just so happy to be home.

"We're going to get drunk and celebrate."

The Ryan brothers told gardai that they were unable to give them information about their 'abduction' although detectives later discovered that they had been kept at a house in Thurles, Co Tipperary, for the week that they were missing.

Searches of this property failed to yield any significant clues and no-one has ever been charged in relation to the 'kidnapping'.

To this day, gardai say they are "very sceptical" about many aspects of the entire saga involving the Ryan brothers.

They were both arrested over the 'kidnapping' but never charged in relation to it.

The alleged abduction story may be bizarre, but what happened in Limerick just six hours before the brothers turned up alive and well showed that the bitter feud really was out of control.

The murder of Christy Keane's brother Kieran on January 29 was directly linked to the brothers' 'disappearance' — and it signalled a new low in the deadly tale of the Limerick feud.

On that fateful afternoon as Keane returned to his Garryowen home after collecting his two children from school, a man was waiting to talk to him.

Kieran's wife Sophie would later recall that man was Dessie Dundon, chewing on a burger.

"They spoke for a minute, at most two minutes, and Kieran came back inside the house, " the widow later told her husband's murder trial.

It has never been proved but it is widely believed that Dundon would have told Keane that he knew where the 'kidnapped' Ryan brothers were located.

He ate his dinner and left soon after in his '02 registered Passat.

That was the last time she saw her 36-year-old husband alive.

Keane called to Owen Treacy's home at 96 St Munchin Street in St Mary's Park at 6.50pm. He asked Treacy to accompany him on a drive and the pair drove across the city to Garryowen.

They eventually found the house they were looking for, 5 Fairgreen, family home of Anthony 'Noddy' McCarthy.

Dessie Dundon and 'Noddy' McCarthy were in the house — 'Noddy' had a .38 handgun in his hand.

Ruthless crime boss Kieran Keane — strongly linked to at least two murders — was stunned. "What the fuck is going on," the crime lord blurted out.

Keane and Treacy had their hands tied behind their backs with duct tape and they were told to sit on a couch. This was now an incredibly serious situation for them.

Their captors asked them to lure their very close associates, brothers Kieran and Philip Collopy, out of St Mary's Park to be set up for murder. Keane and Treacy refused to co-operate.

After a while the pair were bundled into the boot of a Micra and brought to another house. Further efforts were made to persuade them to get the Collopys "out the road".

Then, after a few phonecalls, they were brought down to a garage attached to the house and passed into the back of a Hiace van.

Inside, Christopher 'Smokey' Costelloe had a gun pointed at them. David 'Frog's Eye' Stanners was behind the wheel and James McCarthy was in the passenger seat.

Within 25 minutes, the van came to a stop in Drombanna, outside the city. Stanners took Kieran to the front of the van, pushed him to the ground, stabbed him and then shot him in the back of the head.

Costelloe then began to stab Treacy, until Stanners took the weapon and stabbed him a number of times before leaving him for dead.

Despite being tied up and almost dead, Treacy was able to get help in a nearby house and gardai were rushed to the scene.

Gardai knew that Tracey had vital information to impart.

Detective John Nagle was dispatched to the Mid Western Regional Hospital in Limerick knowing it was almost unheard of for anyone associated with Limerick's feuding gangs to cooperate with gardai.

But Treacy surprised the experienced detective by agreeing to testify against his uncle's killers.

And what he had to say would eventually lead to five of Ireland's most vicious gangland criminals being jailed for life.

Det Nagle later recalled that Treacy was "quite coherent" despite his poor health.

He asked Treacy: "Who stabbed you, and who shot Kieran Keane?"

Treacy slowly replied "a green Hiace" and then said: "David 'Frog's Eyes Fats' Stanners, James McCarthy, Moyross, and Smokie Costelloe."

The three men he was referring to were David Stanners, James McCarthy and Christopher Costelloe.

The Hiace was the vehicle used earlier that night to transfer Treacy and Keane to the isolated area where they were attacked.

This was a crucial early break for gardai, as they knew the identities of three main suspects just hours after the murder.

A senior Gardai source explained: "This was an amazing breakthrough. It made for one of the most exciting nights that I have ever experienced from an investigative point of view.

"It was unprecedented for the exact picture of what happened that night to develop so quickly for the investigation team."

He added: "Det Nagle had vast experience and he knew the situation in Limerick really well. He had to use all his skill when dealing with Owen Treacy in that hospital. It was a real whisper-in-the-ear situation between him and Treacy, as medical staff worked around him trying to stabilise the victim."

Around the same time that Treacy spoke to the detective at the hospital in Limerick, 70 miles away in the town of Portlaoise 'kidnapped' brothers Kieran and Eddie Ryan showed up alive and well.

Meanwhile, once Treacy's health had improved he was able to give gardai the names of the other two men involved in the kidnapping. These were Dessie Dundon and his cousin, Anthony 'Noddy' McCarthy. He also gave a full account of what had happened after he and his uncle were bundled into a van and driven to isolated Drombanna, Co Limerick.

"I was screaming, I was being stabbed rapidly," he told detectives.

Treacy revealed that Christopher 'Smokie' Costelloe had cut his throat with a knife before David 'Frog's Eyes' Stanners "grabbed the knife" and began stabbing him.

He told the detectives that Stanners had said: "This is the last face you're going to see", before sticking the knife into him.

Before this, he had watched Kieran Keane being "pushed to the ground and shot like a dog with his hands tied behind his back" by Stanners.

Thinking that both men were dead, the gang left and Treacy went to tend to his uncle. He saw that Kieran Keane was barely breathing, and went to a nearby house to seek help.

The authorities were notified, and armed detectives arrived at the scene within minutes.

The garda source told this author: "When gardai arrived, Owen Treacy was sitting on the steps of the house while Kieran Keane's body was located in a lonely, dark spot nearby.

"Mr Treacy was in a state of shock and he was covered in blood — it was obvious that he needed urgent medical attention."

Treacy later recalled that when he and his uncle were lured to a house in Fairgreen, Limerick, earlier that night, Dessie Dundon had placed hoods over their heads and taped their hands behind their backs.

Treacy was able to see through the hood, and saw Anthony 'Noddy' McCarthy pointing a handgun at them before ordering them to sit.

Treacy and Keane were then ordered to make a phone call to two of their closest associates — brothers Kieran and Philip Collopy — and get them "out the road", but they refused to do so.

After hearing this version of events, gardai were in no doubt that the plan for January 29, 2003, had been for the McCarthy/Dundon and Ryan gangs to kill all four men.

Such a move would have struck a devastating blow at the Keane/

Collopy gang, who had been feuding with all of the families in question.

Owen Treacy told gardai he and his uncle spent one hour in the house in Fairgreen, during which the men "went on" about getting the Collopys.

After this, Treacy and Keane were brought to another house, before being taken to Drombanna for the planned execution.

The statement gardai received from Treacy was 28 pages long, and they knew his evidence would be indispensable in court.

When Treacy was well enough, he travelled around Limerick with Detective Ger Fitzgerald to point out all the places he was brought to on the night of his kidnapping.

Still in great pain because of his stab injuries, he had severe difficulty moving as he pointed out a dozen different locations.

This was another crucial breakthrough for gardai, as the events of the night started to fit together.

The Garda Technical Bureau found blood at the entrance of a house the two men had been brought to and also on its stairs, thanks to Treacy's assistance.

Another important development for the investigation team came when they searched Anthony 'Noddy' McCarthy's house in Fairgreen, and discovered a Nike cap that Owen Treacy had worn on the night of the murder.

Forensic investigators also discovered blue and red fibres from Kieran Keane's jumper on cushion covers at the house.

A pillowcase found at another property identified by Owen Treacy had duct tape on it, which came from the same roll used to bind Kieran Keane's hands.

Gardai also used the services of a member of Vodafone's technical support staff who was able to corroborate Treacy's account when the expert found that seven phone calls that were made in a house he had been brought to on the night were traced to the nearest phone mast.

The Gardai source explained: "Mr Treacy gave us a very truthful and well-articulated statement which included a huge amount of detail about the events of that night.

"He gave explicit details about the route he had been taken on and there was never any doubt in our minds that he was telling the whole truth."

Meanwhile, after the murder, Anthony 'Noddy' McCarthy and Dessie Dundon fled Limerick for Dublin.

Their car was stopped by gardai in Roscrea, Co Tipperary, but the duo escaped after giving false names.

The traffic gardai in Roscrea had noticed there was something suspicious about the men and later told their colleagues in Limerick about the incident.

This enabled the detectives to track the two men's movements.

Dundon and McCarthy then fled to the UK, but two months later on March 28, 2003, the Gardai received word that the gangland criminals were back in Ireland.

Armed detectives swooped on them in Kilkenny city, where they had been staying with a criminal associate.

Both men again gave false names to the gardai, but this time there was no escape.

McCarthy had even dyed all his hair — including his pubic hair — in an effort to conceal his identity.

The other three men — James McCarthy, Christopher Costelloe and David Stanners — had been picked up by gardai weeks earlier at their Limerick homes, and all five were charged with murder and other serious offences in April 2003.

They would show their contempt for the law upon being charged with the murder.

When Detective Gerry Doherty charged James McCarthy with the killing, the thug replied: "That's only a waste of paper."

And when Detective David Burke charged Anthony McCarthy with the same offence, he replied: "It must be raining murder."

The five Limerick men who were charged and ultimately convicted of the murder of Kieran Keane and the attempted murder of Owen Treacy were Anthony McCarthy (25) of Fairgreen in Garryowen; Christopher Costelloe (24) of Moylish Avenue in Ballynanty Beg; David Stanners (35) of Pineview Gardens in Moyross; James McCarthy (28) of Delmege

Park in Moyross; and Dessie Dundon (24) of Hyde Road in Ballinacurra Weston.

After a dramatic trial at the Central Criminal Court in December, 2003, all five were given life sentences.

Appeals against the convictions were rejected by the Court of Criminal Appeal in the summer of 2007.

During the trial, Owen Treacy was protected by armed members of the Garda Emergency Response Unit on the days that he was giving evidence.

When the five gangland figures were being led away to start their sentences, Anthony McCarthy warned Treacy: "For every action there's a reaction."

And James McCarthy screamed at him: "You will be looking over your shoulder for the rest of your life."

When Kieran Keane's widow Sophie was called into the witness box to give an account of the effect that the murder had on her and her then-teenage sons — the hatred the five convicted killers had towards her was there for all to see.

"Our lives have stopped moving forward," she said. "These men are animals. They took my husband's life for no reason, he never did anybody any harm."

She was then asked what Kieran Keane had worked at.

Before she said anything, the five men shouted: "Selling drugs, killing people. He killed the McCarthys, he killed Eddie Ryan."

After the killers' shouting stopped, she told the court her husband "sold coal", to laughs from the defendants' bench.

Owen Treacy's life remains under constant threat from members of the McCarthy/Dundon gang, but he continues to refuse to enter the Witness Protection Programme.

When questioned about it during the dramatic and tense murder trial, Treacy explained: "I turned that offer down straight away, my lord. I considered it with my family, and considered to stay in my own home. I felt that would be the safest."

He lives in the St Mary's Park area of Limerick, and detectives continue to mount regular operations to keep him alive despite the fact that the McCarthy/Dundon gang was finally destroyed by the

Gardai in special operations between 2010 and 2012.

A garda source said: "It is true that Owen Treacy is still regarded by some as a dead man walking, but we will do everything we can to protect him.

"He was the pillar of the case against those five very serious criminals and the Gardai deeply appreciate that.

"He remained steadfast throughout despite all the intimidation and death threats — which still exist against him to this day."

The murder of Kieran Keane was a watershed in the annals of the bloody Limerick gangland war.

It signalled the end of the dominance of the Keane/Collopy criminal gang and the real emergence of the notorious McCarthy/Dundon gang — despite the fact that five of its most senior members would be locked up because of the murder.

After the bizarre 'kidnapping' that played such a central role in Kieran Keane's murder, Eddie and Kieran Ryan continued to be involved in serious feud related violence.

In July, 2004, Kieran Ryan was jailed for four-and-a-half years for his role in a massive feud-related brawl in a fast food restaurant car park in which the rival factions used golf clubs, a steering lock and pool cues to beat each other.

The brothers are currently locked up – in July, 2010, Kieran was jailed for eight years and Eddie for six when they pleaded guilty to suspicious possession of a high-powered pistol and 15 rounds of ammunition in Limerick two months earlier.

The weapon and ammunition were seized when gardai stopped and searched a car following a surveillance operation in the area.

Limerick Circuit Court was told a member of the Emergency Response Unit sustained serious facial injuries as the men were being arrested.

Time has also not been kind for others who were caught up in the dramatic events of January 29, 2003.

The Collopy brothers — Kieran and Philip — who the McCarthy/Dundons had attempted to lure to their deaths continued to be involved in serious criminality.

Philip's chaotic and dangerous life came to an abrupt end when he died in hospital in March 2009 after he accidentally shot himself in the head with a Glock pistol during a party at his home a few days earlier.

It is believed the father-of-two was showing others how to use the gun and took the magazine out of the Glock pistol but forgot to remove the live round from the breach when he shot himself.

In 2003 he was jailed for two years for violent disorder while in 2007 he and his brother Ray were given a 16-month sentence after threatening to kill another man.

In the months before his death, he was targeted by the Criminal Assets Bureau, which seized a house, two cars and a substantial amount of cash from members of his family.

Just weeks before he killed himself, Philip was a witness in a case at the Circuit Criminal Court in Limerick, where he arrived wearing a bulletproof vest which he showed to the jury.

When asked why he needed to wear it, he replied: "Sure I get shot at every week."

He went on to claim there had been several attempts made on his life in the preceding years.

Meanwhile in May 2011, Philip's older brother Kieran and his younger brother Damian were sentenced to five years in jail each for threatening to kill their former associate Willie Moran.

Limerick Circuit Court heard the brothers believed that Mr Moran owed them money arising out of matters involving their late brother Phillip and horses he owned.

The court heard that Kieran Collopy approached Mr Moran at his home at 9pm on April 14, 2010, shouting about wanting Philip's money back.

Kieran Collopy warned him he better have four or five grand by the end of the night and shouted "I hope you are prepared to die" before striking Mr Moran in the jaw.

Kieran later returned to the house with his brother Damien who threatened to put a bullet in Mr Moran's head.

Also convicted and jailed for eight years in relation to the campaign of terror against Moran was the head of the Collopy family Brian, who was sentenced in February, 2011.

Like many of those sucked into the spiral of violence in Limerick, Mr Moran is under active death threat and has 24-hour armed garda protection.

CHAPTER 4

He Signed His Own Death Warrant

There were many similarities between Daniel Gaynor's death and the brutish life that the 25-year-old criminal had led — it was extremely violent, particularly horrible, and savage almost beyond words.

Gaynor — a notorious gangland figure with a string of previous convictions who was the chief suspect for two murders as well as the attempted murder of an innocent postman — was gunned down in broad daylight as he walked with his young family on St Helena's Road in Finglas at 6.50pm on August 14, 2010.

It was a sunny, balmy evening and the execution happened while children played on the street and people sat in their gardens.

Finglas at that stage was the gangland murder capital of Ireland but this gun killing was especially barbaric even by the standards of the troubled north Dublin suburb, which had been plagued by a reign of terror instigated in the main by gang boss Eamon 'The Don' Dunne who had been shot dead in a Cabra pub four months earlier.

Gaynor was targeted as he walked down the street with his partner Sarah Treacy and his two children, who were aged just six and seven-years old when they saw their dad shot in the neck and then saw him bleed to death on the roadside.

Gaynor was walking with his family when a gunman ran up and blasted him from behind. The killer escaped over a railing down to the Tolka Valley estate, where he had a getaway vehicle waiting for him.

A local woman later recalled that her mother and siblings were just yards away when the shots rang out on that warm Saturday evening.

"They were only after going round the back when they heard three shots going off and they ran around and my ma saw the blood coming out of his mouth," she said.

"His kids were there with his girlfriend and the kids froze — they didn't cry or anything but the girlfriend was saying, 'Don't leave me, don't leave me.'"

The young woman said she knew Gaynor's family.

She said: "Our kids played football with his kids, they were the same age. That [the shooting] will be with them for life now."

In her statement to gardai Gaynor's partner Sarah Treacy, who had been in a relationship with him for exactly two years on the day he was shot dead, told detectives they were walking with his two children toward their aunt's house to drop them off.

She said she saw a silver gun with a barrel on it and "thought it was someone messing".

"Daniel tried to turn his head to the left," said Ms Treacy, who added she did not know how many shots there were as she was "deafened".

"I just heard a ringing in my ear and Daniel fell in front of me."

She said she "could just see a pair of eyes" but saw the person was wearing a peaked cap, a white glove "like a magician's glove" and a gun.

Ms Treacy said she saw a person of slim build between 5ft 8in and 5ft 11in "running towards the Den" after the shooting.

She said she went over to where Gaynor was shot and tried to get her mobile phone to ring the emergency services.

He was taken to hospital and after 20 minutes to half an hour her boyfriend had died.

While Gaynor was dying in hospital, the scene of the shooting was swarmed by gardai and after getting a detailed account of where the gunman had run off to, the officers got a massive break within minutes.

A garda source explained: "We got lucky — the gunman screwed up big time. We came across a virtual DNA goldmine."

Detectives could barely believe their eyes when they discovered a gun, glove, hat and hoodie discarded at Gortmore Road.

The discovery was made by Garda Peter O' Connor of Finglas Garda Station, who later examined a Sturm Ruger gun which had three empty cases and two live rounds. He also found a white glove, a black Street Magic baseball cap and he retrieved a McKenzie hoodie from a hedge at Gortmore Road.

Rarely in the history of Irish gangland had a killer been so sloppy after carrying out a murder but the investigation had a very long way to go.

The backdrop to Gaynor's murder was a very dangerous feud that broke out in the summer of 2010 between members of the Real IRA led by their slain leader Alan Ryan (32)and a gang controlled by a millionaire former Provo from Dublin who made his fortune smuggling illegal cigarettes into the country for over two decades.

The secretive veteran gangster has been a long-term target of the Criminal Assets Bureau and spends his time between Dublin and Spain where he owns a massive villa.

With strong republican credentials, he had previously co-existed with the Real IRA but a row over money led to a bitter dispute that became so intense gardai received intelligence that one side was plotting to blow up an entire pub in a massacre — similar to bombings seen in the North during the Troubles.

At the time, Ryan's reinforced Real IRA were stepping up campaigns of extortion against other criminals and they wanted their cut of the lucrative illegal cigarette market that cost the State €526m in unpaid taxes in 2011 alone.

As the dispute turned into a bitter feud in the summer of 2010,

Gaynor was hired as a hitman by the Real IRA faction and this would ultimately lead to his death.

There can be no doubt that he had the vicious criminal pedigree to be used as a hitman for hire.

Gaynor was just seven years old when his own father, Robert McGrath, was shot dead.

In that case, however, it was by gardai, who foiled an armed post-office raid by McGrath's criminal gang in Co Meath in 1992.

By the time Daniel Gaynor was 21 years old, he had served a number of jail sentences for serious crimes such as firearms offences and witness intimidation as well as dealing in cocaine and diazepam.

He was 19 when he was jailed for six years for firing a gun through the window of a house because a teenager living there owed him just €100.

Gaynor carried out the attack because he wanted his money back in order to buy his girlfriend a Valentine's Day present.

Just a year later, Gaynor was handed a further two years in jail for intimidating the 62-year-old woman whose home was attacked in the shooting.

In that trial, the court heard how Gaynor approached the woman while she was waiting at a bus stop and told her that her son's days were numbered.

He then made a gesture to her with his fingers in the shape of a gun and as he moved away shouted that her son was "f***ing dead".

The woman had to be placed in a witness-protection programme and the family was forced to move house, such was their fear of Gaynor.

He had also built up a reputation as a hitman-for-hire and after being released from jail in 2008, Gaynor was involved in a number of shooting incidents on behalf of the IRA.

Gaynor, originally from Berryfield Drive, Finglas, was the chief suspect for shooting innocent postman Robert Delany at his home in Tallaght in October 2008.

Mr Delany was sprayed in the face with lead pellets from a shotgun blast and remains in a permanent vegetative state at Peamount Hospital in Co Dublin.

The postman was targeted after he broke up a row involving dangerous criminals from Tallaght with IRA connections.

Daniel Gaynor's younger brother Robert Gaynor was jailed for 20 months in February, 2012, for stealing the car that was used as the getaway vehicle in the tragic shooting of Mr Delany.

Daniel Gaynor was also questioned about the stabbing murder of Maurice Martin (21) in Finglas in June 2009.

Originally from Finglas but living in Co Meath, Mr Martin was stabbed on the street after a party. His remains were found on a grass verge at the junction of Cardiffsbridge Road and Tolka Valley Road.

A mobile phone video taken just weeks before Gaynor was murdered, showed him at his brutish worst and showed why so may people were in fear of the violent thug. In the video-clip, which lasts just 20 seconds, Gaynor attacks a young man who he accuses of hitting his child.

During the sickening attack, Gaynor smashes punch after punch into the young man's head before he falls on the ground.

And then, in a disgusting display of thuggery, the suspected gangland assassin jumps on the young man's head before kicking him a number of times in the head.

In the video, Gaynor can be heard screaming in a high pitched Dublin accent: "Don't ever, ever kick my f**king kid again" and when his victim pleads for the attack to end, Gaynor shouts: "You have not had enough; you haven't had enough until I say you have enough" as he continues to kick him in the head.

Eventually Gaynor's friends who videotaped the sick attack on their mobile phones call Gaynor away from the young man who is left on the ground in agony.

A source explained: "What's on that videotape was typical Daniel Gaynor. He was a huge fella and he handed out plenty of hidings like that during his short life."

By July, 2010, tensions between the Real IRA faction and the

West Dublin mob were spiralling out of control.

A source explained: "There was a major stand-off over money — neither side was backing down.

"It was very tense — the Special Detective Unit as well as armed detective units throughout Dublin had to increase patrols on the streets.

"At one stage — intelligence came in that one faction wanted "a spectacular" — they were planning to get a huge bomb and commit mass murder of the other side."

So when the Real IRA wanted to murder someone to teach the Dublin crime boss a severe lesson, they turned to Daniel Gaynor — a young criminal with a terrifying criminal pedigree.

Gaynor remains the chief suspect for murdering Colm 'Collie' Owens (34) who was shot dead at the Corn Store, an animal feed warehouse, on the Grove industrial estate at Dubber Lane, Finglas, on July 9, 2010.

But it was a killing that was akin to signing his own death warrant.

Owens was targeted simply because he was on very friendly terms with the Dublin crime boss. He was not considered a major criminal and came from a decent family.

Gardai believe that it was Gaynor who pumped at least six bullets into the head and body of the 34-year-old dad-of-one who was shot dead because of a feud in which he was not directly involved.

A source explained: "The RIRA just wanted to get at the older fella — they knew that murdering Owens would drive him nuts. They knew it would make him feel vulnerable."

And it did. The crimelord — who can't be named for legal reasons — decided he would try and massacre the brothers who control the Real IRA in Dublin — dangerous dissident terrorists who are heavily involved in extortion, gun-crime, murder and other serious, organised crimes.

The veteran Dublin mobster was closely linked to Ireland's most prolific gangland killer Eric 'Lucky' Wilson — but with Lucky locked up in a jail in Spain's Costa del Crime after he killed an English criminal in a pub there earlier that summer, the crime lord is believed to have turned to one of Lucky's most trusted men, his older brother John Wilson.

Everyone knew that the Real IRA gangsters regularly socialised at The Players Lounge pub in Clontarf, north Dublin and the plan seemed simple enough — get John Wilson to approach the pub, shoot the dissident republicans, and flee the scene in a VW Golf that had been stolen earlier.

But the volatile criminal – who was later shot dead in Ballyfermot in 2012 – was an inexperienced gunman and he completely botched the job.

Instead of shooting the intended targets, senior Real IRA men including Alan Ryan from Donaghmede on Dublin's northside, Wilson almost murdered three completely innocent people on the night of July 26, 2010.

It would be another 26 months before Alan Ryan would be shot dead and this would be part of a completely separate feud with Coolock based drugs gangs.

Innocent doorman Wayne Barrett (32) survived the gun attack despite having a bullet lodged in his brain.

As well as shooting the innocent doorman, two customers standing outside were also shot in the incident — Austin Purcell (24), from Marino, was shot in the chest, while his friend Brian Masterson (30) was shot in the back.

Both have recovered from their injuries.

The shooting took place around 12.30am at the pub, which is on the corner of Fairview Strand and Philipsburgh Avenue.

Mr Barrett was outside the front door of the premises and four or five customers were chatting nearby when the gunman ran across the road.

Dressed in a balaclava and dark clothing, the gunman opened fired with two handguns before he reached the pub.

His target was apparently Mr Barrett, who was shot in the head and slumped to the ground immediately.

But the gunman continued firing and the two customers were also hit in the shooting spree.

"It was like something out of the wild west," a witness said.

The outrageous incident at The Players Lounge pub in Clontarf showed that the feud between the shadowy West Dublin-based crimelord and the Real IRA was completely out of control.

When his plot to wipe out the dissident republican bosses at the Clontarf pub failed so spectacularly, he turned his attention to Daniel Gaynor who he blamed for murdering his friend 'Collie' Owens.

After the debacle at The Player's Lounge, he turned to another associate of Eric Wilson — his younger brother Keith, then aged 22, who had just nine previous convictions for minor offences.

However, gardai considered the wannabe gangster to be "a very dangerous criminal" who had been mentored by his older brother.

Eric is currently serving a 23-year sentence in a Spanish jail after being convicted in July, 2011, of the murder of Englishman Daniel Smith who he shot 11 times including in both testicles after a row over a woman at the Lounge Bar in Riviera del Sol near Fuengirola in June, 2010.

He was on remand in prison on this charge two months later so the Dublin crime lord decided that using his younger brother for the murder of Gaynor would be the next best thing.

After all, Keith had idolised and was mentored by Eric who is three years older than him when the brothers had their dysfunctional and crime-ridden upbringing at their home on Cremona Road, Ballyfermot.

Significantly, gardai believe Eric and Keith Wilson had worked together on at least one gangland murder before Daniel Gaynor was shot dead.

This was the murder of drug-dealer Anthony Cannon (26) who was shot multiple times in the head in broad daylight while being chased by a masked gunman in July, 2009, on St Mary's Avenue West, Ballyfermot.

The man who gardai suspect shot Cannon is Keith Wilson who is believed to have received detailed phone instructions from his older brother in the minutes before the shooting happened.

It is believed that Eric 'Lucky' Wilson — linked to up to 10 gangland murders — was based in Spain when Cannon was murdered but he enlisted his younger brother to carry out the hit.

No-one has ever been charged with that murder which means it was a successful gangland assassination — but things were not to run so smoothly for Keith just 13 months later when he murdered Daniel Gaynor.

It is believed that Wilson spent a number of days staking out Gaynor before he finally struck on that sunny Saturday evening in August 2010. When he observed Gaynor walking with his family at St Helena's Road, it did not bother the gangster that there were innocent people including two children with him.

He approached him from behind and fired three shots at Gaynor — one of the bullets went straight into his neck, a fatal injury.

Wilson ran away to a getaway car and was driven at speed from the scene. But when he discarded the gun glove, hat and hoodie, it gave gardai the opportunity to build a massive case against him.

Within hours of the murder, Keith Wilson was on a flight to Spain where he was put up in the villa owned by the veteran Dublin gangster who had ordered the hit.

As with every murder, a huge investigation started and gardai were not only helped by the forensic value of the items that Wilson had recklessly dumped on the ground.

Because the feud had been causing so much concern for a number of weeks, the secretive Crime and Security branch of the Gardai had tapped into a number of phones of those involved.

This, combined with the fact that detectives in Ballyfermot Garda Station had intimate knowledge of the workings of the veteran cigarette smuggler and his gang, meant that in the space of less than 48 hours, Keith Wilson had been identified as the chief suspect.

Meanwhile, a post mortem conducted on Gaynor's body by deputy state pathologist Dr Khalid Jabbar determined that he died from a single penetrating gunshot wound to the neck.

Detailed tests were carried out on the gun that was recovered near the murder scene.

Ballistics specialist Detective Garda David O'Leary discovered that the bullet taken from Mr Gaynor's neck was too badly damaged to link it to a Sturm Ruger SP101 revolver found near the scene.

The bullets he received for examination were made of plain solid lead and they had no copper or metal surround.

Det Gda O' Leary later told Keith Wilson's murder trial, that there were three discharged cases, one live and one misfired.

"In my opinion the order would have been one misfire and three discharges — audibly, a click and three bangs," he told the court.

He said the shells discharged had been from that kind of firearm but it was not possible to say if it came from that particular weapon.

Det Gda O' Leary said there were holes in the gun as the last digits of its serial number had been drilled.

He explained that if you drill through the metal you cannot retrieve the digits whereas if it is filed off it is possible to do so.

Det Gda O' Leary also said a gun with drill holes in it would leave an impression on the bullets it discharged.

He said the bullet found in Gaynor was similar to the bullet in the live round found in the gun.

As August turned into September in 2010, gardai continued to gather more and more information on Keith Wilson as they listened in to phone calls and got information from secret criminal informants. They were left in no doubt that he was the killer.

The investigation was also helped by more sloppiness from the killer. As he enjoyed a party lifestyle in the Spanish villa, officers were able to trace his exact location after photos of the hitman were posted on Facebook.

The murder of Gaynor had led to a huge increase in garda activity surrounding the players in the feud and it is believed that at some stage in the autumn of 2010 a truce was called between the West Dublin crimelord and the Real IRA.

It is not known how much but it is thought that one faction paid the other a considerable sum of cash to bring an end to gang hostilities.

In the meantime, a number of the senior Real IRA figures had been arrested by gardai investigating the murder of drug dealer Sean Winters (42) in Portmarnock, north Dublin, in September, 2010.

Winters was shot a number of times and died outside the gated Links apartment complex in Portmarnock, where he lived — his murder was not linked to Gaynor's death.

Meanwhile there can be little doubt that murder is bad for business in gangland and making money is of course the main aim of the RIRA faction as well as their West Dublin rival.

It is not known if he kicked Keith Wilson out of his Spanish villa but when Wilson returned to Dublin on a flight from Spain on the night of Sunday, November 7, 2010, the gangster barely had a cent on him.

Gardai had received specific intelligence that Wilson was coming home and a team of detectives from Finglas Garda Station were waiting for him at Dublin Airport where Det Sgt Alan Brady arrested him at 11.30pm.

Wilson was brought to Finglas Garda Station where he typically refused to co-operate with the investigation team and would not even agree to provide a DNA sample.

However on the Monday morning, Wilson smoked a cigarette at the back of the station during a break from questioning.

When he put it out, detectives recovered the cigarette butt and immediately preserved it and sent it off to the State's forensic lab so it could be tested for DNA recovered off the four items that Wilson had discarded at the crime scene.

A source explained: "It certainly was an unconventional way to get DNA from an uncooperative suspect and there was some concern that the DPP might not find it acceptable or that a judge might not agree with it but in the end we were able to charge Wilson."

Wilson's DNA was recovered on all the items which led to forensic scientist Dr Clara O' Sullivan later finding that the chance of someone having the same DNA was less than one in a billion.

The gardai had their man and at 10.27pm on Tuesday, November 9, 2010 — less than 48 hours after he was picked up by armed officers in Dublin Airport — Wilson was charged with Gaynor's murder.

Wilson replied "no comment" when charged by Det Sgt Alan Brady in the station and he was brought to Blanchardstown District Court the following morning where he was formally charged.

Wearing blue jeans and a grey T-shirt, Wilson stood with his arms folded and remained silent during the brief proceedings, was granted legal aid and remanded in custody.

It was Keith Wilson's first time in jail and sources say that he hated life on the inside.

On January 6, 2011, Wilson tried to get bail but was unsuccessful after gardai received intelligence that he would try and escape the country.

Refusing bail in the High Court, Mr Justice Patrick McCarthy said he had not been impressed by the evidence of Wilson who told the court he had been very close to his late grandfather.

Judge McCarthy said he did not accept that Wilson had been particularly close to his 85-year-old grandfather.

He refused to release Wilson for an eight-hour spell to attend the funeral despite an offer by his family to post €5,000 bail just so he could be there.

Wilson told his barrister Seamus Clarke he was very close to his grandfather and used to clean his house for him. He said he wanted to attend the funeral and had no intention of skipping bail.

In cross-examination by Ms Grainne O'Neill, counsel for the Director of Public Prosecutions, Wilson said he could not remember his late grandfather's address but knew where the flats were where he had lived.

He could not remember the exact number of times he had visited his grandfather during 2010 but felt it would be about 10 times.

Wilson agreed with Ms O'Neill that his grandfather had been in a home since February 2010 and said the 10 visits must have taken place during the months of January and February last year.

When asked if he spent a lot of time in Spain he said he had and could not remember the number of times he had been back and forward to and from Spain last year.

Ms O'Neill told Wilson his evidence to the court was "simply not credible".

Detective Inspector Martin Cummins told the court he had opposed the granting of bail before a previous High Court bail hearing and he did not believe Wilson would turn up to face trial.

"No amount of money would ease my mind as to the concerns and risks of this man getting bail," Det Insp Cummins said.

Judge Mc Carthy said he had previously dealt with applications for compassionate bail in which there were special circumstances involved. He refused to release Wilson who, the judge said, had made a very poor impression in the witness box.

Wilson went on trial in late October, 2011, for the murder of Daniel Gaynor, with the killer offering no real defence — instead relying on the prosecution to prove their case.

But with such strong DNA evidence, he never stood a chance of being cleared.

Prosecuting counsel Alex Owens told the jury that the case relied "very heavily on silent witnesses and circumstantial evidence" and "all of the circumstantial evidence points to the guilt of the accused".

He added: "Either he's the unluckiest man in Ireland or he is drowning in a sea of circumstantial evidence." A jury at the Central Criminal Court took just under three hours to reach a guilty verdict.

A statement read to the court on behalf of the family said Mr Gaynor's two young sons, who both witnessed the killing, are deeply traumatised and are now in counselling.

His girlfriend Sarah Treacy is also in regular contact with a counsellor, the court heard.

It was also heard that the victim's mum is inconsolable and his family would never be able to get over it.

Mr Justice Garrett Sheehan said he had no discretion in sentencing for the murder and handed down the mandatory life sentence on November 8, 2011.

Wilson showed no emotion as the judge also imposed an eight-year term for firearms offences to run concurrently with the life sentence.

The trial was marked by intimidation with some of Wilson's associates in court attempting to intimidate gardai.

In one incident, while the jury were deliberating on a verdict in the case, a close associate of the killer made a sinister threat to a senior detective in court.

"Wilson's pal approached the detective and made some threatening remarks — he also indicated that he knew where the garda's mother lived," a source said.

Tensions were high in the Central Criminal Court before the jury were sent away to deliberate after the dramatic two-week trial and gardai had major concerns when a number of supporters of Keith Wilson arrived in court to hear the closing speeches in the case.

"They were acting in a fairly threatening and intimidating manner and at one stage there were major worries that one of them would get up and start shouting stuff in front of the jury that could cause the entire trial to collapse.

"This carry-on looked like it was being orchestrated by the man who made the threat to the detective.

"At one stage, he kept coming in and out of the courtroom and he was making and taking lots of calls on his mobile phone," a source explained.

Ultimately closing arguments were made without any major incident but sources believe the speed of the process caught Wilson's crew by surprise.

While he showed no emotion in court, Wilson was sickened that he was now facing the rest of his days behind bars.

Just weeks after the guilty verdict, Wilson went ballistic and wrecked a holding cell after prison officers caught him with an illegal mobile phone in the B wing of Mountjoy Prison.

After the phone was seized, prison management decided that Wilson should be transferred out of the jail to Portlaoise Prison for a two-month period and he was placed in a holding cell in Mountjoy while preparations were made for his departure.

But the feared gangland thug "went mental" when he discovered that he was going to be sent to the maximum security Laois jail.

"He was in the holding cell on his own and smashed the place up. He clearly didn't want to be sent to Portlaoise and he was very angry that he was caught with the phone.

"He went absolutely mad — he had to be removed by a control and restraint team and put on the van to be taken to Portlaoise," explained a jail source.

With Keith and Eric Wilson both now serving life sentences and in custody since 2010, Ireland has seen a major decrease in gangland assassinations.

While, of course, the jailing of the two notorious brothers is not the only reason for this drop in gun murders, gardai believe it is "significant."

The West Dublin crimelord who is suspected of ordering Daniel Gaynor's murder is still operating and still a huge target for gardai.

In 2011, his crew got involved in a completely separate feud with the Continuity IRA which led to one murder and a number of shootings. But this feud has also now ended.

The Real IRA gang that Gaynor had worked for in the murder of the crimelord's friend 'Collie' Owens is still one of the most active and feared crime organisations in the State.

CHAPTER 5

Cracking The "Perfect Crime"

Gardai spent three tense years trying to nail sly wife-killer Joe O'Reilly. In what was probably the most high-profile murder case in our history, it has become a cliche to say that O'Reilly thought he had committed the perfect crime — but he was very wrong.

The murderer would not be rotting behind bars right now except for one of the most detailed and wide-reaching Garda investigations in our history.

During the lengthy investigation, it seemed like gardai were playing a deadly game of cat and mouse with O'Reilly, as certain details of their probe were leaked to the media just to see how he would react.

There has never been a murder case that received so many column inches and by the time O'Reilly's appeal was dismissed at the Court of Criminal Appeal on March 6, 2009, the entire country was aware of Joe's family background, his personal relationships and those of his slain wife Rachel's relatives.

But this was no cheap soap opera. It was the horrific tale of a pretty mother-of-two being savagely murdered by her own husband in their home.

The cold facts of the case are that on the morning of October 4, 2004, Joe returned from his workplace not long before 11am to the home he shared with Rachel and their two sons, then aged just two and four — and he brutally battered his wife to death.

Rachel suffered a dreadful ordeal, receiving several blows to the head with a heavy blunt instrument which has never been found.

Her blood-soaked body was discovered by her mother, Rose Callaly, in the bedroom of the house in The Naul, north Co Dublin.

At first, Joe O'Reilly was not considered a suspect — but within hours his strange behaviour and weird answers to Garda questions led to experienced officers becoming extremely suspicious. And they quickly realised they were not dealing with a botched burglary.

Ultimately, a huge investigation kicked off involving hundreds of officers led by Michael Finnegan, the former Chief Superintendent of the Louth-Meath Garda division, and retired Assistant Commissioner Martin Donnellan, backed up by some of the most experienced and talented detectives this country has ever had.

This heavyweight line-up of Garda top brass was also backed up on the ground by experienced officers such as Detective Sergeant Pat Marry (now Detective Inspector), who got O'Reilly to admit he was having an affair with his mistress Nikki Pelley.

Another key figure was Detective Sean Fitzpatrick, who trawled through hundreds of hours of CCTV footage and identified O'Reilly's car driving to and from the house.

Among the problems that gardai confronted were that after Joe murdered his wife, he trashed their bedroom to make it look as if a burglary had taken place.

Officers believe that he then had a shower to wash Rachel's blood off himself, changed his shirt and then went back to work at the Broadstone Bus Depot on the northside of Dublin city.

At this stage, O'Reilly must have been thinking that his plan was working perfectly — no one apart from him had a clue that there was anything wrong until just before 1pm, when Rachel failed to collect her children as arranged at a creche in Swords.

So the devious thug hatched the next part of his plan — despite murdering her only two hours earlier, he rang Rachel's mobile.

He left a message saying: "Hiya Rach, it's only me, I just got a call from Helen in Montessori.

"She says you haven't picked up Adam. Give us a shout. I'm going to try the home number. You've no doubt left your phone at home or in the back of the car or something."

At 2pm, the cold-hearted killer rang Rachel's mother Rose feigning deep concern and asked her to call out to the house in The Naul to check on Rachel while he went to the creche to pick up his children — who had been left waiting for over an hour.

While Joe made a point of hanging around the creche for 20 minutes more than he needed to, Rose had the extremely grim task of coming across her cherished daughter lying in a puddle of blood with appalling head injuries.

A senior detective who investigated the case told this author: "I can't stress enough the state that he left her in and the horrible death she suffered. He really crucified that woman — she was absolutely savaged."

Joe's callous actions have sickened detectives to this day — speaking in the aftermath of O'Reilly's failed murder appeal on March 6, 2009, retired Assistant Commissioner Martin Donnellan said: "When you consider the amount of planning that O'Reilly had carried out, the meanest thing he did was to make sure Rachel's body was found by her mother, Rose Callaly.

"He hung around the school until he was certain Rose had found the body and that was absolutely appalling and a despicable act."

But this was not the brazen killer's only despicable act. When he finally arrived back at The Naul, he made a point of hugging Rachel's body which meant that he was covered in her blood.

By doing this Joe made sure that DNA would never be a major strand of evidence in the case against him.

People who know Joe say that he is a very arrogant man — and in this case his arrogance worked very heavily against him.

When gardai arrived at the scene, the killer was quick to say "I have probably destroyed the forensics" when he admitted hugging his wife's corpse.

He might have been right about that, but seasoned gardai also know that this is not a regular comment to come from a grieving husband so they decided to dig deeper.

When questioned by detectives on the night of the murder, O'Reilly gave his version of the day's events.

He stated he had left early that morning, went to the gym and then to Broadstone Bus Depot, where he spent the morning. He claimed his work colleague Derek Quearney could confirm this.

O'Reilly had no idea at this stage that two-and-a-half years later at his murder trial in the Central Criminal Court, Mr Quearney's evidence would show that this alibi was far from watertight.

In the weeks after Rachel's murder, the investigation intensified and O'Reilly started to make big mistakes.

First he appeared on The Late Late Show with Rachel's mother Rose to appeal for information about the murder — and the icy body language between the two raised eyebrows among the public across the country.

Just days later, O'Reilly did sit-down interviews with a number of newspapers at his home, where he admitted that he was a suspect in the case. Suddenly the case was being talked about in every pub and hair salon in the country.

While O'Reilly tried to play the media, in the background gardai were building a massive case against him.

As the media circus continued, officers made 7,000 different enquiries, conducted 5,000 interviews and viewed thousands of hours of CCTV footage.

O'Reilly had openly admitted he was having an affair with Dublin advertising executive Nikki Pelley, but claimed this was over at the time of the murder.

Mobile phone evidence would later show that there was a total of 18 communications between the unsuspecting Nikki and Joe on the day of the murder, including 58 minutes and 25 seconds of actual talk time.

The first call between Ms Pelley's and O'Reilly's phone was made at 5.45am on the morning of 4 October 2004, the day Rachel O'Reilly was murdered.

Phone records provided to gardai by mobile phone provider O2 indicated that a 27-minute phone call was made from Ms Pelley's home to Joe O'Reilly's mobile at 5.45am.

Figures obtained by gardai showed that calls between the two phones at different times on that morning lasted in total for almost one hour between 5.45am and 8.46am.

Gardai were acutely aware that most women who are murdered are usually killed by their partners.

Now the serious stuff started — and this involved checking phone records and internet communications. What turned up in this trawl ultimately cracked the case.

Detectives were able to establish that O'Reilly's phone had bounced a signal off a mobile phone mast at 9.25am and 9.52am at Murphy's Quarry half a mile from his home — this was around the time Rachel was murdered.

Previously, O'Reilly had told gardai that he was at the Phibsboro bus depot during that time which experts have now placed his phone in north Co Dublin.

And crucially, O'Reilly had also told gardai that his mobile phone was in his possession at all times on the day of Rachel's murder.

Ultimately, when the case went to trial, an O2 engineer was able to show the jury what parts of the city O'Reilly had communicated with on his mobile phone.

He showed how Joe's phone signal moved from his workplace near the Nangor Road, through Chapelizod, out on the M50 motorway, on to the M1 and to Murphy's Quarry, near his home, up to 10am on the morning his wife was murdered.

The phone signal then made its way towards Dominick Street in Dublin's north inner city, and back out towards Joe's workplace.

The O2 engineer showed the jury a separate presentation with both O'Reilly's phone and Mr Quearney's phone.

Of major significance was the fact that their phone signals were coming from different parts of the city at a time when O'Reilly said the men were together.

The mobile phone angle to the investigation was something that gardai were always very conscious would be a very useful tool, and it was something that O'Reilly was grilled about when he was first arrested on November 17, 2004.

During his first interview, which started at 11.40am, O'Reilly was asked about his mobile phone.

When asked: "You had it with you all day?" he said: "Yes, I think so."

Det Sgt Sean Grennan then asked him whether he had the mobile with him when he answered it. He replied: "Yes."

Asked: "You're not denying killing Rachel." He replied: "I deny killing Rachel."

While Joe denied and continues to deny murdering Rachel, it was mobile phone technology which ultimately snared him.

Speaking about the mobile phone breakthrough when the case was finalised, retired senior garda Martin Donnellan said: "This has been a landmark case in relation to the use of mobile phone evidence in a criminal trial.

"It has now been accepted by the courts that mobile technology is tried and trusted and found to have been accurate.

The senior investigator added: "O'Reilly claimed he was nowhere other than Broadstone in Dublin that day, but mobile phone evidence absolutely proved he was out in Balbriggan and came back in.

"He sent a text message to his wife, who was then deceased, shortly after 9am and the message started at one mast and finished at another closer to the city, which indicated he was on his way back from Balbriggan."

But things were to get even worse for wife-killer Joe.

A series of hate-filled emails that he sent to his sister Ann in the months before the murder revealed the pure contempt that O'Reilly felt towards Rachel.

Gardai got the emails when Detective Gerry Keane went to O'Reilly's offices at Viacom in October 2004 and seized his laptop.

The detective was also given a CD containing a number of Joe's personal work files and folders after producing a search warrant at the work premises.

Included in these emails was Joe's admission that his marriage was effectively over. "Me + Rachel + Marriage = over!!!", he even declared in one email.

In a bitterly sarcastic tone, he called his late wife "The World's Greatest Mum", and even used abusive language such as "c**t" in relation to her.

In another email, he sneered at her attempts to organise a "romantic dinner" for the two of them.

Tellingly, O'Reilly told his only sister in another email: "By all means, drag her fat ass outside and kick it into the middle of next week, but not in front of the boys, and don't leave any marks that can and will be used against you in a court of law."

Gardai also found another email in O'Reilly's sent folder on the morning of October 4, 2004, the day his wife was murdered.

It was sent to Kieron Gallagher, a friend of the killer, who O'Reilly was due to meet for lunch that day. O'Reilly told Mr Gallagher in the email: "I will be out and about most of the morning, and in poor phone coverage areas, so unless I hear otherwise from you, lunch at 2pm, usual place?

"Got the 40 quid off my brother at the weekend," he added.

The blandness of these sentiments on the morning that O'Reilly was to murder his wife shocked investigators.

Separately, as the net closed in on O'Reilly, gardai placed a tap on his phone — something which the cunning killer seemed to be aware of and he started having false conversations in an attempt to take them off the scent.

A month after the murder he made a call to his wife's mobile phone for much the same purposes. "Hi Rach, it's Joe. I'm really sorry for the very, very early phone call," he said, knowing that he was really talking directly to gardai.

"This time a month ago you were probably doing what I'm doing now, getting the kids ready for school. But now you're so cold. But the sun is out. It was just a normal day but you had less than two hours to live," he added.

Now O'Reilly was truly caught in a cyber trap and gardai knew they had their man — so when they arrested Joe at 10.20am on November 17, 2004, they also picked up and questioned his lover Nikki and Derek Quearney, the man who the killer wrongly thought could provide him with a cast-iron alibi.

When questioned by detectives, Nikki admitted that Joe had referred to his wife Rachel as a "wasp" or a "c**t".

She also admitted that Joe had spent the night with her after his sensational appearance on The Late Late Show on October 22, 2004, where he appealed for information about the murder.

Quearney did not provide O'Reilly with the alibi he wanted.

Joe remained as cold as ice while being questioned, even when confronted by the mobile phone evidence.

Former senior detective Michael Finnegan later recalled: "O'Reilly never changed his demeanor. He is a very cool man — he really was convinced that he wouldn't be charged."

Meanwhile, the main result from the CCTV investigation — which saw three dedicated gardai studying thousands of hours of footage — showed a car matching the description of O'Reilly's Fiat Marea near the family home on the morning of the murder.

The results from the CCTV investigation were sent to a specialist lab in the UK where they were analysed.

Later, forensic imagery analyst Andrew Laws would tell O'Reilly's trial that there was "moderate support" for the belief that a car seen passing a quarry less than a kilometre from the O'Reilly home was the same make and model as Joe O'Reilly's navy blue Fiat Marea estate.

And the UK-based expert also said there was 'strong support' for the belief that a car seen passing a premises eight kilometres south of the O'Reilly home was the same make and model as O'Reilly's car.

Mr Laws compared footage of cars seen passing Murphy's Quarry and the Europrise premises at Blake's Cross on the day of the murder, with footage of a reconstruction conducted by gardai using Joe O'Reilly's navy blue Fiat Marea estate.

Murphy's Quarry is 850 metres from the O'Reilly home, and Blake's Cross is eight kilometres away.

Mr Laws used three techniques or 'tests' when viewing the footage.

The first test compared the general measurements of the cars in the different pieces of footage to see if they corresponded.

The second test compared specific features of both cars for likenesses or differences, while the third involved using video technology to superimpose one car onto another to check for similarities.

O'Reilly was finally charged with murder on October 20, 2006 but he did not go on trial until late June 2007.

On the morning that he was charged at Swords District Court, up to 40 photographers, cameramen and reporters stood waiting at the court after word spread like wildfire that the DPP had finally agreed there was enough evidence against him.

The accused man arrived from Balbriggan Garda Station in a van at approximately 11.30am. Dressed in a green fleece, navy tracksuit bottoms and dirty trainers, he was met by a wall of photographers, all pushing for the best angle.

There was a brief scuffle when onlookers moved forward to catch a glimpse of the accused man. Some shouted words of abuse as he was led inside the courthouse.

Reporters followed O'Reilly inside, filling the courtroom and receiving a reprimand from Judge Patrick Brady, who said that people talking in the court would be removed, no matter who they were.

After two other cases were adjourned, Det Sgt Patrick Marry gave the court details of when and where the accused man was arrested and charged. The proceedings took no more than three minutes before the judge granted an application to remand him in custody.

O'Reilly sat in the dock chewing gum throughout the brief appearance without speaking. When he emerged, men and women in the crowd cursed at him as he was bundled into the van headed to Cloverhill Prison.

Twelve days later O'Reilly was granted bail and he lived with his two sons and mother up until his trial started just over eight months later.

The trial finally started in late June 2007 and after a marathon case that kept the nation spellbound, the killer was finally convicted of murdering Rachel on July 21, 2007.

However, this was not the end of the agony for Rachel's family as Joe appealed his murder conviction almost immediately.

In the appeal, heard in December 2008, counsel for O'Reilly argued that evidence of mobile phone records and data relating to the location of O'Reilly's mobile phone on the date of his wife's murder should not have been permitted by the trial judge to go before the jury.

It was also submitted there was no evidence before the court that O2 Ireland was a licensed phone operator under the terms of the Postal and Telecommunications Service Act 1983 and therefore the phone evidence was not legally before the jury.

It was also argued that emails from a computer alleged by the prosecution to be O'Reilly's should have been excluded because their evidential value was outweighed by their prejudicial value as they were sent in June 2004, several months before Rachel's death. It was argued that the time was too far removed from the events of October 2004.

It was also submitted the trial judge should not have allowed evidence of three interviews with O'Reilly while in Garda custody to go before the jury in a manner where, he said, it was clear to the jury he had remained silent for the most of the time he was being interviewed.

A witness statement by O'Reilly from October 6, 2004 should also have been excluded because he was at that stage a suspect, he claimed.

The trial judge had erred in allowing that statement to be used as evidence because O'Reilly had told gardai some weeks later the contents of that statement were correct, it was argued.

It was further argued that evidence relating to CCTV footage about movements of cars on the date of the murder was inadmissible and flawed as it only involved comparisons with a Fiat Marea car, the type of car driven by O'Reilly, and no other car.

Thankfully for Rachel's family this appeal was rejected on March 6, 2009, with the court dismissing every strand of the appeal.

But in the aftermath of the Court of Criminal Appeal's decision, Joe's mother Ann revealed that her son intended to bring a further appeal to a higher court but, at the time of going to press, no date had been set for a Supreme Court appeal.

Joe himself backed this up in September 2009 in letters he wrote from prison which were published in the now defunct *Star on Sunday* newspaper.

"I'm focused and determined to prove my innocence and the truth will come out, please God," O'Reilly wrote.

"As for the Supreme Court appeal — yes, unfortunately that will take a bit of time, but please God, it'll be worth the wait."

The killer brazenly claimed that the evidence against him was botched.

He wrote: "The Mobile phone stuff!! Very confusing and very technical.

"Basically, the DPP alleged, successfully obviously, that my phone-cell was placing me closer to my house than to where 'I said' I was which was Phibsboro.

"Now, there is so much wrong with that, I don't know where to start.

"However, I'll leave you with these thoughts/questions.

"Have you ever had a dropped call or have you ever lost your signal?

"Have you ever stretched your arm 800 yards down a hill, past a door, through two doors, turn left, through a kitchen door, turn right down a hallway, left into a bedroom, kill someone, then leave the way you came without being seen?

"No? Me either. But I have dropped a call and I have lost a signal. So, hardly water tight technology eh?"

O'Reilly is described as a model prisoner in the Midlands Prison and over the years he has been meeting for prayer sessions with a religious leader in a bid to save his soul.

The murderer has been regularly visited in the jail by Isaac White, a Jehovah's Witness called 'the pastor' by inmates.

O'Reilly, who converted to the faith from Catholicism, was having prayer meetings in jail for hours every month at one stage.

As Joe languished in the Midlands Prison, his next bid for freedom happened in August 2012, but it was again quickly thrown out of court and was truly bizarre and brazen in nature.

Mr Justice Michael Peart dismissed Joe's application to the High Court for a declaration under Article 40 of the Constitution that his detention in jail was unlawful. Mr Justice Peart said that, according to an affidavit, O'Reilly had served an application to have his murder conviction quashed.

O'Reilly told the court he had been unable to engage the services of a solicitor and was dealing with his application through the post, while pursuing an application for legal aid.

He had written to the court claiming his detention was rendered unlawful by the fact that he had had more restricted access to the courts than other citizens, and was disadvantaged by not being permitted to attend personally.

But Mr Justice Peart said O'Reilly had been lawfully sentenced, meaning a restriction of certain rights.

"One of those restrictions is one of which this applicant complains, namely that unlike other persons who are not in prison he may not simply walk into court and move an application or attend the Central Office to file papers," Judge Peart said.

The judge said that this did not mean O'Reilly was denied access to justice — he could still make applications by post.

Judge Peart said the grounds put forward by O'Reilly that his detention was unlawful had no possibility of success and he dismissed the application.

While O'Reilly does everything in his power to win back his freedom and the country remains fascinated by the wife-killer, there can be no doubt that his actions have had a devastating effect on the Callaly family.

The family was struck with another dreadful tragedy. In September 2010, Rachel's beloved sister Ann lost her brave battle against cancer at the age of 31.

Ann had provided huge support to her parents Jim and Rose

during the terrible murder ordeal and had always been there for her family but less than five months after Joe was convicted she started getting treatment for a tumor behind her eye — which ultimately killed her.

Ms Callaly's last public appearance was in November 2009 when she sat alongside her father in the audience of The Late Late Show during an interview with her mother — who had just published her own book about the murder.

At the time Ann talked about how her health had suffered as a result of the stress of her sister's murder. Earlier in 2010, in a show of support for their sister, Anthony and Paul Callaly had their heads shaved to raise funds for the Irish Cancer Society.

At that time Ann said she was very proud of her brothers.

"I'm so blessed with such a supportive family and great friends," she added.

Speaking in the aftermath of Ann's tragic death, her highly respected dad Jim said: "We are absolutely devastated. She put up a great battle, a great struggle. She really thought she could beat it.

"She was a wonderful daughter and a wonderful woman. She is with Rachel now. She will be buried beside Rachel. We have had a steady stream of visitors. This is a very difficult time for the family but we're all very close."

Even though Joe remains defiant, the gardai who helped to nab him are in no doubt that they got the right man.

One of the main investigators in the case, retired detective Michael Finnegan, explained: "It was a very intensive investigation but really worthwhile. We are particularly pleased for the Callaly family. They are a lovely family and from what we heard Rachel was a lovely woman."

Mr Finnegan hailed the quality of technical evidence that gardai gathered in the case.

"The signal from O'Reilly's phone was coming from half a mile north of the phone mast at Murphy's Quarry. His home is half a mile north of the quarry," he explained.

"The Swedish company dealing with the phone mast information was excellent but it was a slow process.

"It was probably the first case of its type built on so much technical evidence from phone traffic and emails. Even though it was circumstantial we believed the evidence was compelling."

Mr Finnegan added: "We are pleased that our investigations stood up under intense scrutiny by the prosecution, judge and the jury.

"The result was very worthwhile. Even though it was circumstantial, the Gardai always believed we had our man."

These sentiments were backed by another top investigator, Martin Donnellan, who said: "Attention to detail and real determination by the team is crucial to getting a conviction.

"I must compliment the investigation team. From the most senior to the most junior, they all acted very professionally.

"This was a team effort and there were no stars in the investigation. Everybody played their part, from the local gardai in Balbriggan to the rest of the Garda personnel in the Dublin North division, the NBCI and the Technical Bureau."

But while gardai and the vast majority of the people of Ireland are absolutely certain that prison is where Joe deserves to be, he still has his supporters and these include his immediate family as well as his lover Nikki Pelley who all still regularly visit him in prison.

In an interview aired on TV3 in May 2012, his older brother Derek spoke out, saying: "The Joe I know isn't a scumbag, he isn't a wife-beater and he most definitely isn't the Devil. My definition of the Devil is the ultimate evil and the Joe O'Reilly I know is anything but the ultimate evil.

"In my mind I've never had reason to think ill of him, it just isn't in his physical or mental make-up to take anyone's life.

"I know my brother, that's all I can say, I just know my brother."

Speaking about the high-profile trial which dominated the headlines for months, Derek said: "We got back to the house one day and got ourselves together and I sat him down and I said, 'Tell me now, look me in the eye — have you got anything to do with this?'

"And his look was like he had been stabbed with a poker, his eyes welled up and he goes, 'How could you even ask me that?' I believed him and I've never had a reason to doubt since.

"The whole thing was just a complete and utter circus. People were bringing packed lunches with them, flasks and drinks and sandwiches — it was like they were going to the movies.

"When you were leaving the courts at the end of the day's proceedings you were hearing people driving past and shouting obscenities at you.

"You just try your best not to respond to it. Sod's law being sod's law, if you replied somebody would take a picture and send it to the paper.

"So you are walking along, biting your lip and trying not to say anything. It's not easy, but we did it. It was a horrible time and I don't ever want to go through anything like that again — nobody would I ever wish anything like that on, nobody."

While Derek was content to do that TV interview as well as an exclusive interview in the *Sunday World* newspaper where he expressed the same sentiments, Joe's lover Nikki was never happy with the limelight despite being regularly photographed on special occasions as she made prison visits to her lover.

In May 2012, Nikki received an estimated €75,000 settlement after *The Sun* published her letters to him in jail.

The breach of privacy action by Nikki Pelley, who is from Rathfarnham, south Dublin, was settled after the letters were published on March 19 and March 21, 2011.

Ms Pelley had sought an injunction, damages and declarations against the newspaper.

As Joe O'Reilly faces into his sixth Christmas behind bars, the murder he committed continues to fascinate the public while it still leaves Rachel's family completely heartbroken as they contemplate all they have lost.

As they still grieve, Joe can at least count on the loyalty of his family and lover as he continues his quiet life in prison.

But the bad news for him is that some commentators believe he may never be released from jail considering the massive profile of the 2004 murder and the controversy it caused.

CHAPTER 6

Death Of A Schoolboy

When a lively 11-year-old schoolboy went missing close to his home it seemed he had vanished into thin air.

The country watched in horror as teams of volunteers searched for young Robert Holohan in the rolling countryside around the east Cork market town of Midleton.

The weather and atmosphere were dark and gloomy on January 4, 2005 — even more miserable than is usual in Ireland at that time of year.

Robert's disappearance sparked one of the biggest investigations of recent times, with a Garda team led by now retired Superintendent Liam Hayes backed by the elite National Bureau of Criminal Investigation (NBCI).

The event was a media frenzy, with much speculation that the schoolboy had been abducted by a paedophile.

Eventually, after a massive eight-day search, Robert's body was found on January 12 in undergrowth at Inch Strand, 12 miles from his home.

The body had been mutilated by animals and had decomposed so badly that dental records were needed to confirm Robert's identity.

Who knows what was going through the head of Cork IT

student Wayne O'Donoghue at this time? The then 20-year-old had been Robert's friend and neighbour, but also his killer.

Later he took part in the searches five times and had lied to Robert's mother Majella when she asked him for information.

But what O'Donoghue did not know was that gardai were already building a strong case against him.

He would crack four days later — the day after he and almost the entire town attended Robert's emotional funeral at Holy Rosary Church in Midleton.

When O'Donoghue — who was released from prison in January 2008 after serving three years of a four-year manslaughter sentence — finally decided to confess, it took a marathon 13 hours for him to tell his version.

He went into great detail as two experienced officers — local detective Michael O'Sullivan and NBCI Detective Sergeant Peter Kenny — listened intently to his story.

O'Donoghue was already the prime suspect, and gardai would have pounced on him in less than 48 hours if he had not come forward.

A senior source close to the investigation explained to this author that O'Donoghue had become a suspect up to five days before he confessed.

Our source said: "In any missing person case, questionnaires are filled in and many people are informally questioned.

"In O'Donoghue's case, he was questioned at least four times and he was asked to give a fingerprint sample, which he agreed to willingly.

"The reason that we went back to him again and again was because he had admitted early on that he had an argument with young Robert on the day he went missing and we were not satisfied with the version of events he gave during these informal questions.

"Crucially, he had no alibi for a two-hour period that day and no real explanation for where he was — this was very important as it was during that time period that we estimated Robert Holohan had been taken.

"Wayne's behaviour when he was involved in the searches was

also something that had made us suspicious and it meant that we started paying him much closer attention.

"On at least one occasion he had acted in a very agitated way on the search and even gave a couple of senior gardai a tongue lashing when it was decided to finish searching in a particular area one evening."

The gardai that O'Donoghue acted aggressively towards were the late Detective Inspector Martin Dorney, who was later promoted to the position of superintendent, and Inspector Brian Goulding (now Detective Inspector), two of the most experienced gardai in Munster.

But if Robert's body had never been found it is unlikely O'Donoghue would ever have been arrested.

A Garda source explained: "In virtually every homicide case, if there is no body there will be no charges."

It was mobile phone technology which gave gardai a rough location for Robert's body through a process called triangulation.

"When Wayne disposed of Robert's body at Inch Strand, he also disposed of the young lad's Nokia 3200 mobile phone at the scene and switched it off," our source explained.

"The triangulation process recorded this and after some time Robert's phone sent out a signal to a local phone mast and this enabled us to get an approximate location of where the phone was."

When gardai worked with mobile company O2 to track Robert's phone, they saw another mobile had been used at Inch that day — it was later found to belong to O'Donoghue.

Records from O'Donoghue's phone company proved that he called Robert's mobile phone at 9.19pm and 9.39pm on the day he was killed — when the boy had been dead for hours.

When O'Donoghue was later asked by officers why he made the calls, he replied: "To keep up the pretence."

He was then asked if he had left a message or heard the phone ring out. He answered: "I don't know, to be honest. I wasn't really listening."

O'Donoghue also confirmed to gardai that a photograph found on Robert's mobile phone was of a poster which was hanging on

O'Donoghue's bedroom wall. The phone showed the photograph was taken at 7.32am on the morning of December 28.

The poster, which bore the words 'Student Crossing', showed a cartoon version of a black and amber road sign with a figure crawling across the road on his hands and knees, carrying a pint glass.

Asked by gardai if he had taken the photograph and texted it to Robert on his mobile, O'Donoghue replied: "I never did but I witnessed him taking that picture and there was also someone else in the room while he took that picture as well."

The case against the student became even stronger after Robert's body was discovered.

The massive search was in its eighth day when two local volunteers, Tom Deady and Martin Sloane, were detailed to walk up each side of a road near Inch Strand in east Cork.

"I looked into the ditch. I noticed a leg. There was no shoe on it," Mr Deady later told gardai.

A Garda technical expert, Detective Thomas Carey, said that he found burn marks on the hem of Robert's T-shirt and on the waist band of his underpants and tracksuit bottoms, as well as scorch marks on twigs from the scene where Robert's body was dumped.

White plastic bags had been used to cover the upper half of the body and forensic investigators found two fingerprints which later matched samples from O'Donoghue. These were a right index fingerprint and a middle left fingerprint.

Forensic expert Detective Pat O'Brien made the match around the same time O'Donoghue was coming clean at his home with detectives Michael O'Sullivan and Peter Kenny.

The veteran officers spent almost 13 hours in the house as he confessed in the presence of a solicitor.

Our source pointed out: "Those lads did a great job there — they used all their training and experience to put Wayne at his ease.

"It was during this very lengthy conversation that Wayne admitted that he decided to tell the truth after reading an article in the *Star on Sunday* newspaper that morning.

"It is my understanding that a senior member of the

investigation team passed on information to the paper because he thought Wayne might read it that morning. It was a brilliant ploy to encourage him to try to give himself up.

"The article made it clear that gardai were treating the death as a tragedy, and that there had been no sexual motive involved.

"It also gave a lot of clues about who the suspect was. When Wayne read some of the detail in it, he knew it referred to him."

O'Donoghue confessed how on the fateful day of January 4 he had refused to drive Robert to the McDonald's in the town because he was working on a college assignment.

He said Robert then walked out of the house and went to pick up his bicycle in the driveway — but as he did so, he began tossing pebbles at O'Donoghue's Fiat Punto car.

Robert threw some more pebbles that hit O'Donoghue on the head, he said.

"Robert, will you ever grow up?" he shouted, grabbing the boy's neck and jerking him away from the car.

"I released the grip with my right hand, but I was still holding him by the scruff of the neck with my left hand," O'Donoghue claimed.

"Nothing was said between us at this stage. I then moved my left hand up to his Adam's apple and said, 'Will you stop with the f***ing stones?'

"I can't describe how tight I held him. I don't know how long I held him, but it seemed very short. I didn't intend to cause him any harm.

"When I removed my left hand from his throat, he just fell to the ground."

In chilling detail, O'Donoghue also described what happened immediately after he killed Robert.

He said: "I had no problem lifting him. I laid him on the bathroom floor.

"I said, 'Oh my God what did I do?' At this stage I believe he may have been dead. I was really panicking and I knew my mother and brother were due back shortly.

"I came back into the bathroom again, hoping he would be

standing up. He wasn't breathing."

Then in graphic detail O'Donoghue revealed how he planned to kill himself when he returned to the kitchen.

The statement read: "I took a black-handled knife out of the drawer. My idea was to cut my throat. I went to the bathroom.

"I can't explain my actions at this time. I was looking at Robert. I looked at the mirror and held the knife close to my throat. I threw it back in the drawer. I was panicking and I decided I would have to remove the body."

O'Donoghue then wrapped his young victim's head and legs in black plastic bags.

He continued: "I picked up the body. Robert was light and easy to carry." He put the body in the boot of the car and put Robert's BMX on a seat.

Before driving off, he called his girlfriend Rebecca Dennehy and said: "I will be down in a while."

O'Donoghue continued: "I put the bike in a ditch on my right-hand side. I was driving fast. I was shaking, I didn't know where to go. I pulled into Jim Foley's garage.

"I was sitting in the car in a daze wondering what I would do now. I bought a bottle of Lucozade and got back into the car."

O'Donoghue said he headed towards the remote Inch Strand beach. He added: "I drove very fast. I came to a roundabout. I just kept flying. I travelled along the road, headed in the direction of the beach.

"I could then scan the beach. I also saw a car. I knew then I couldn't leave him on the beach."

He finally dumped the body at 5pm. He said: "I was driving slowly back. I threw the body into the ditch. I did all this very quickly. I was in a state of panic. I was upset. I wanted to leave the scene."

O'Donoghue said he first tossed one of Robert's black runners that had come off into the heavily brambled site.

His statement told how he returned to the family home he shared with his parents and two brothers and tried to pretend nothing had happened.

He said: "I rang Rebecca because she would be wondering where I was. I drove over to Rebecca's. The Simpsons were on. I hadn't a clue what I said to her. I hadn't a clue.

"I was thinking how disrespectful it was where I had put the body and how I could do that to a friend. I decided I was going back down.

"I knew I had to maintain a normal routine. We played the PlayStation in my room."

It was then that frantic Majella Holohan phoned as she searched for Robert. O'Donoghue added: "I knew it was her when it rang. I dropped Rebecca home. I came back."

O'Donoghue went on a 25-minute torch-lit hunt to find the body which he intended to move to the beach and he had brought petrol to burn plastic bags near the body.

His statement continued: "I then started talking to the body saying 'Robert' as if he was alive. I couldn't get the bags out because it was in bushes and nettles.

"I poured some of the petrol from the bottle on to the black plastic bags. The bag was only partially lit. I could see a leg. Then I saw his body was legs up and head down.

"I knew from the position of the body I wouldn't be able to get it out from where it was. I decided to return home to keep some normality. I decided to put off the suicide until I had put the body on the beach at first light."

He returned to Ballyedmond and sat watching the American TV show The Swan with Rebecca. He said: "I knew this might be the last time I saw Rebecca as I was planning to commit suicide. I was keeping up appearances."

By the time he returned home, the search for missing Robert was going into full swing. O'Donoghue added: "I went out searching for the night with my brothers. As each day went by I felt it became more difficult to make my plan to remove the body. Every day it seemed harder and harder.

"I wish to say I'm deeply sorry for what happened. Robert was like a brother to me. If I could switch roles I would. What happened was a fluke, an accident."

O'Donoghue also maintained there had been nothing improper in his relationship with Robert.

The following day, O'Donoghue went through his statement again at Midleton Garda Station, where he was asked to identify a number of items that had been seized in the investigation.

These included Robert's BMX bike, which he had cycled up to the neighbouring O'Donoghue family home on the day he died.

There were runners found with the body at Inch Strand, some 11 miles from where they both lived, in Ballyedmond, outside Midleton. There were also plastic bags, which the gardai noted were found with the body.

The reward for the large crowd who braved the cold weather outside Midleton Courthouse on January 17, 2005, was their first glimpse of the young man accused of one of the most publicised killings in modern Irish history. Emotions were running high, and some of the crowd screamed abuse.

Inspector Brian Goulding gave evidence that he had formally charged Wayne O'Donoghue under Section 4 of the Criminal Law Act with the killing of Robert Holohan at Ballyedmond on January 4. Goulding told the court the student had replied: "I have nothing to say."

For the duration of the hearing O'Donoghue kept his head bowed, only looking up briefly at his family.

O'Donoghue never applied for bail, and was to remain in the Midlands Prison until his four-year sentence for Robert's manslaughter ended in mid-January 2008.

The four-year jail sentence upset Robert's family and the child's mother felt so strongly about it that she wrote to the DPP to complain.

In the letter, which was sent to the DPP two days after O'Donoghue was sentenced to four years for Robert's manslaughter, Majella Holohan queried some of Mr Justice Paul Carney's comments about her son's injuries during the sentencing hearing.

In particular, she expressed concerns over both Mr Justice Carney's comments that Robert's injuries were "at the horseplay end of the scale" and over the weight that Mr Justice Carney appeared to attach to medical evidence called by the defence.

Medical evidence had been given on behalf of the defence by Professor Jack Crane, Northern Ireland's chief pathologist, who agreed with the State Pathologist, Professor Marie Cassidy, that Robert's death was "an asphyxial type of death related to some pressure or force being applied to his neck".

But Mrs Holohan pointed out in her letter to then DPP James Hamilton that Prof Crane had never examined Robert's body but based his findings on notes and photographs taken by Prof Cassidy, who carried out the post-mortem.

She also expressed concern that Mr Justice Carney made no reference to injuries to Robert's mouth as well as bruises on his back and buttocks and on the inner surface of his fourth and sixth ribs and to soft tissues over the rib cage identified by Prof Cassidy.

In July 2006, the DPP appealed against the leniency of the four-year sentence handed down to O'Donoghue and also argued that the sentence did not recognise O'Donoghue's attempts to divert the focus of the Garda inquiry away from him.

But in October 2006, the Court of Criminal Appeal refused to increase the sentence.

In a controversial 33-page judgment, the court dismissed the DPP's claim that the sentence was too light.

The three-judge Court of Appeal ruled that forensic evidence didn't conclude that 11-year-old Robert died a violent death and that Mr Justice Paul Carney didn't undervalue the gravity of the offence.

The court ruled that it was acceptable for Mr Justice Paul Carney to describe the altercation between the killer and Robert as "at the horseplay end of things".

It also stated that O'Donoghue's cover-up was taken into account when sentencing him, and that the judge was right not to allow Majella Holohan's powerful victim impact statement to affect O'Donoghue's sentence.

Mrs Holohan sparked a public outcry in January 2006 at the sentencing hearing when she claimed in her victim impact statement that traces of semen had been found on her son's clothing — an issue which had not been mentioned in the trial.

Mr Justice Paul Carney later responded to Majella's claims during a high-profile speech in which he said: "By the time I got to my chambers the word 'semen' was already on the airwaves and the accused was being branded as a paedophile killer, which he was not, and which the Director of Public Prosecutions never suggested he was.

"Nobody would have wished to add to the grief of the victims but they were given an iconic status by the media, in particular by the tabloids.

"The victim was acting under the influence of obsessive grief. The tabloid press do not have this excuse."

Although Wayne O'Donoghue was sentenced to four years, at one point it looked like he would face a life sentence.

In April 2005 he was charged with murder after a controversial new DNA technique, called low copy number DNA, used by British forensic scientist Dr Jonathan Whitaker established that semen found on Robert's left hand was not dissimilar to O'Donoghue's DNA.

He had tested a swab taken from Robert's palm and compared it with a DNA sample from O'Donoghue.

On foot of his report, the DPP directed that O'Donoghue be charged with Robert's murder.

Our source explained: "There was a sense when the first results came back that there was a strong case for murder."

But when samples of material taken from O'Donoghue's bathroom mat were later sent to Dr Whitaker, they were not identical to the semen from Robert's hand.

This sample led him to express doubts about his first report, leading the DPP to decide that the sample should not be introduced as evidence.

Separately, a report from a leading British forensic science laboratory supported O'Donoghue's insistence that nothing improper took place between him and Robert. O'Donoghue has always contended that the tiny trace of semen found on

Robert's right hand was innocently transferred from the bath mat to Robert's hand when O'Donoghue placed him there while trying to revive him.

A Garda source said: "We realised that the DPP was going to withdraw this evidence.

"There is a feeling the DPP should have introduced a new charge in relation to Wayne moving Robert's body. If convicted of this Wayne would surely have been given a bigger jail sentence."

Not surprisingly, O'Donoghue lived a very quiet life in jail and was described as a model prisoner.

In April 2006, he gave his only ever media interview and it was with Conor McMorrow of the now defunct *Sunday Tribune*.

O'Donoghue explained that, no matter where he was, his mind was constantly focused on one day: January 4, 2005.

"I cannot say how sorry I am for everything that happened to the Holohan family. I never stop thinking about what happened. I think about it 24/7. I just keep thinking: why did this happen to me? Why did it happen to Robert?" he told the *Sunday Tribune*.

"It was just a normal day like any other day. I had spent the morning studying for college and I had been visiting my girlfriend earlier as well. When Robert came to the house it happened. It all happened so quickly. He threw a handful of pebbles at my car and one of them hit me on the back of the neck. That's what happened. It was over in seconds."

"I think about the Holohan family a lot, as they have lost Robert out of all this. I cannot say how sorry I am for everything that has happened to them. I think that, by getting a four-year sentence, I was treated fairly by the courts, but this is not a four-year sentence, this is a life sentence. I will feel sorry for what I did until the day I die."

Speaking about the cover-up and the fact that he did not come clean immediately after Robert's accidental death, O'Donoghue said: "Had I been thinking any way logically, I would have rung an ambulance or the gardai but panic set in. I dragged Robert into the house to the bathroom and tried to get him back. I laid him out on the floor in the bathroom and even though I didn't know what I was doing, I lifted his right hand to check for a pulse."

He vehemently denied that a tiny trace of semen found on Robert Holohan's body belonged to him.

"I am not a paedophile. That semen was definitely not mine, and I couldn't believe when people started to say that there was anything going on between us," he said.

When O'Donoghue was released in January 2008, it was front page news in all national newspapers for days on end.

As some commentators expressed outrage at the coverage, it was *Evening Herald* editor Stephen Rae who explained why O'Donoghue's release demanded so much attention in the media.

Mr Rae said that, as far as he was concerned, O'Donoghue "forsook his right to privacy when he killed Robert Holohan. (His) solicitor (Frank Buttimer) has put out the feeling that it's the media who are out to get Wayne.

"We're not out to get Wayne. All we want from Wayne is answers. There were questions that weren't answered in the court which still remain to be answered."

O'Donoghue is now a free man — but he has rarely been seen in public in Ireland since his release, and his solicitor Frank Buttimer has said it is unlikely he will ever be able to lead a normal life in this country.

With this in mind, O'Donoghue began a new life abroad when he started a new college course in England in the autumn of 2008.

He enrolled in a degree course in Architectural Technology at Leeds Metropolitan University and was photographed by a number of newspapers enjoying boozy nights with his new girlfriend Sara.

He completed his course and now works as a professional in the city of Leeds, where he uses the first name Paddy.

As O'Donoghue picks up the pieces of his life, little Robert's heartbroken parents Mark and Majella and siblings Emma and Harry are still struggling with the tragic events of January 2005.

But the couple did get some much-needed joy in their lives in October 2008, when Majella gave birth to a baby girl in Cork.

Born a week overdue, baby Sadhbh Mary weighed in at just less than 9lbs.

But they will never get over the pain of what happened — sentiments they expressed in November 2011, when two newspapers settled a libel action with Wayne O'Donoghue over their coverage of the murder case, meaning the killer got a big payout.

A year earlier, TV3 made a settlement with O'Donoghue over the same libel issue. All parties who were sued by O'Donoghue acknowledged that the semen that was found on Robert's body did not belong to Wayne.

Speaking after the court case in November 2011, Mark Holohan described the justice system as "a joke" and said the pain over his son's death will never leave his family.

Mr Holohan said he and his wife were "still haunted by the terrible events" surrounding Robert's death.

"We have to try and go on but it is always with us," he said. "But the pain of losing Robert will never go away."

Mr Holohan said he remains convinced that his son did not receive proper justice over the circumstances of his death.

Many of the gardai who played an important role in the Wayne O'Donoghue investigation have since retired, but the officer who was absolutely central to the case died in the most tragic of circumstances in January 2011 at the age of 51.

Hugely respected, very brave and highly dignified to the very end, Supt Martin Dorney was buried with full Garda honours after he died from an aggressive form of skin cancer.

His illness had been misdiagnosed by his GP, Dr Pat Lee.

His GP had removed a suspicious mole from his leg in 2003, but had failed to notice a lab recommendation that a wider area around the mole be excised.

In March 2009, Supt Dorney was diagnosed with malignant melanoma.

The diagnosis came just 12 months after he had been promoted.

Supt Dorney's cancer diagnosis sparked an Irish Medical Council (IMC) fitness-to-practise hearing against Dr Lee.

In July 2010, the fitness-to-practise panel recommended the

suspension of Dr Lee for three months. But the IMC later doubled it to six months.

Dr Lee later admitted he feels personally responsible for the pain and suffering that the Dorney family endured.

"I feel a profound sense of anger and shame in myself for having allowed this situation to develop," he said.

"It was never my intention or my belief to cause this. How I wish this had never happened," Dr Lee added.

In his last interview about the misdiagnosis, Supt Dorney said that he was "staring down the barrel of a gun".

"It is too late for me but I just hope it is not too late for somebody else," he said. "I am not vindictive or bitter but I am concerned that this situation could reoccur and affect other patients in the devastating way that it has affected me.

"Dr Lee has apologised to me personally and I have accepted his apology," he added.

CHAPTER 7

The Scissors Sisters

Irish detectives took the drastic step of consulting African voodoo experts about a murder as fear gripped the force that a sadistic ritual killer could be on the loose in Ireland.

Gardai spoke to South African black magic experts after the horrific discovery of the badly-dismembered limbs of an African man floating in the Royal Canal in Dublin on March 30, 2005.

The body was unidentifiable, and at the time there were around 60 African men on the missing books.

As the mystery deepened, rumours began to spread around the capital that a sinister cult may have performed a brutal sacrificial killing.

At first it seemed that the case was similar to the discovery of a dismembered body in London's River Thames four years earlier.

But as the days went on, gardai began to see the first leads surface — and one piece of evidence emerged as potentially crucial in their bid to identify the victim.

An Ireland soccer jersey had been dumped with the remains. Gardai hoped it would help identify the murdered man.

They decided to focus on Dublin's African community in an appeal for information — and Mohammed Ali Abu Bakaar from Somalia read the appeal in *Metro Eireann*, a popular newspaper with our African community.

He told gardai he believed the body may have been his friend, 38-year-old Kenyan national Farah Noor, saying he hadn't seen him since St Patrick's weekend.

Noor was an extremely violent individual who was in a dysfunctional relationship with a Dublin woman called Kathleen Mulhall who he had met in a Tallaght nightclub in 2001.

Kathleen would later claim that she was beaten by him every day and that he used to put out cigarettes on her body.

Bakaar revealed he had seen Noor, his girlfriend Kathleen, and her daughters Charlotte and Linda Mulhall in Dublin city centre on St Patrick's Day, all drinking heavily.

Bakaar said he was with his girlfriend when he last saw Noor on O'Connell Street on Sunday, March 20.

Noor was with his girlfriend, whom he knew as "Katherine", and her two daughters. He said: "I called him to talk to him because I knew after a few drinks, anything could happen to him."

He said he went to tell his friend to go home and relax. As he was talking to him, Kathleen came up to stop him and told him: "Just leave him alone, he's OK."

He said this happened between 5.30pm and 6pm and he remembered his friend had been wearing the Irish away soccer jersey with green and white stripes.

Over a month later, Bakaar said he was reading the *Metro Eireann* newspaper for the African community when he saw an article about the body of somebody of African origin being found in the canal.

He said there was a picture of a T-shirt and socks. "I just thought Farah used to wear this T-shirt and I rang people to see if they had any contact with him," he added.

He later tried to ring a number for Noor but someone answered and hung up.

Investigations later established that this phone was sold to a man by John Mulhall — the father of Charlotte and Linda.

At first the names meant nothing to gardai — but they were soon to become synonymous with one of the most violent murders ever perpetrated in Ireland.

At this stage, detectives had already tried to establish the victim's identity through isotope analysis, which was undertaken by a forensic scientist who was based in Belfast.

From examining the density of the victim's bones and the minerals present, the scientist was able to determine with near certainty that the dead man had lived in the Fitzgibbon Street area for the last six months of his life.

As a result of the information supplied by Bakaar, detectives were able to find the house of horrors where Noor met his gruesome end at Richmond Cottages in north inner city Dublin, and to establish that there had been no sign of him there since early March.

Forensic officers found only tiny specks of blood in the house. But the blood they found matched the canal remains, and after several weeks they confirmed that they had identified the body.

This meant detectives could now conclude that Farah Noor had been murdered at the Ballybough flat.

A post-mortem examination showed that he had been stabbed a total of 22 times — 18 in the middle of his chest.

Pathologist Dr Michael Curtis observed that 20 stab wounds were to the front of the body and two were to the back. The wounds had caused injury to the heart, stomach, liver, lungs and one kidney.

During dismemberment, soft tissue of the body had been cut "cleanly" but the bones had been severed "relatively clumsily by repeated chipping from an instrument such as an axe or a cleaver".

Dr Curtis noted the head and neck had not been recovered and the penis had also been amputated.

He recorded the probable cause of death as penetrative wounds to the trunk of the body, but he said that he had not been in a position to take into account the significance or otherwise of any injuries to the head.

Meanwhile, gardai were able to make contact with Noor's family in Kenya and DNA proved that the body was him.

Almost immediately, Charlotte and Linda Mulhall — the

daughters of Noor's girlfriend Kathleen — became chief suspects.

After all, CCTV images obtained by gardai showed the sisters just hours after the murder walking through Ballybough with Noor's dismembered body in their sports bags.

The footage from supermarket security cameras showed them walking in silence in the wind-driven rain, meeting few passers-by at 7am on the fateful day.

But frustratingly for the dozens of officers involved, at that point nothing directly linked the sisters to the murder.

And despite canvassing and interviewing hundreds of residents in the Ballybough area, no-one was able to provide any meaningful information. But that was all about to change.

A major breakthrough happened in July 2005 when the sisters' brothers John and James contacted the investigation team from Wheatfield Prison — where they were serving short sentences — and gave gardai crucial evidence about the case.

The investigation, led by experienced Detective Superintendent Christy Mangan, continued to gather crucial evidence throughout the summer of 2005.

And by August 3, the team was finally in a position to make arrests — and Charlotte and Linda, who were later to be dubbed the Scissors Sisters, were arrested and taken in for questioning. Also arrested were the sisters' parents Kathleen and John.

At first there were no admissions — but, unknown to gardai at the time, Linda Mulhall had been suffering from psychotic episodes and terrifying flashbacks ever since the grisly murder of Noor.

After all, she had spent hours cutting up Noor's body with her sister Charlotte in the flat before helping her sister dispose of the body parts.

She even had to live with the fact that she buried his head in a park in Tallaght.

A source close to the Mulhall family told this author: "Both sisters lost the plot in a major way — they were always big into drink and drugs, but they were abusing these substances like never before after the murder."

The warm summer day of the arrests must have seemed a long time since cold March when the brutal murder was carried out.

Linda and Charlotte had spent a lot of the time since on crazy alcohol binges, trying to block out the memories of their crime.

The investigation team treated the Mulhalls with great care.

Detectives listened carefully to their denials and different accounts of where they were on the day of the murder, March 20.

After 12 hours the four Mulhalls were released without charge.

Although gardai were sure of the sisters' involvement, they didn't have enough to go on — but the tide was turning against Charlotte and Linda.

Detectives got their first lucky break on the morning of August 17, when Detective Sergeant Liam Hickey received a very unexpected call from John Mulhall Snr, the sisters' father.

He was wracked with guilt and told the officers he needed to talk to them.

Det Supt Mangan and Det Sgt Hickey met him in a south inner city laneway and listened intently as John explained that his daughter Linda knew where Noor's head was hidden.

He went on to assure the officers that Linda would tell the truth about everything.

After this meeting, the senior gardai felt a real sense of relief that the case was finally going to be cracked.

That night they drove to the Mulhall family home at Kilclare Gardens in Tallaght but Linda was not there. It later emerged that she had been hospitalised after cutting her wrists.

Two days passed before they returned to confront Linda — but she refused to talk. The optimism the detectives had felt just days earlier began to wane.

But events were to take a further unexpected turn when Linda and her law-abiding sister Marie had a bust-up at their home — which ended with Marie threatening to call the gardai to tell them exactly what happened in the flat on March 20, 2005.

Linda took things into her own hands, making a hysterical call to Det Supt Mangan to tell him that she needed to speak to him.

The detective was shocked at this turn of events, especially when

Linda said she was prepared to talk about the murder.

Det Supt Mangan and Det Sgt Liam Hickey drove out to Tallaght again and were directed to a bedroom where Linda was sobbing.

Eventually she composed herself and told the officers the grim story of what had really happened five months before.

The detectives had finally got the breakthrough they had worked so hard for, and as they listened to Linda's confession they knew they could now charge the 'Scissors Sisters' with murder.

Det Supt Mangan later recalled: "We were very taken aback. We were hours with Linda and she gave us a full statement.

"It was quite surreal sitting there listening to what she was telling us, between talk of her making dinner for the kids and the like."

After this first confession, gardai travelled to the house in Kilclare Gardens a number of times to get further statements from the dysfunctional mother-of-four.

In December 2006 — after Linda was given a 15-year jail sentence for manslaughter and Charlotte was given a life sentence for murder — one source close to the investigation spoke of Linda in almost sympathetic terms.

The source said: "The place was spotless. Linda would be ironing or washing clothes or looking after the kids. She was cooperative but extremely upset, as you can imagine.

"We asked her to recount the story and she did, in all its gruesome detail. Once she decided to cooperate, she cooperated fully.

"I don't know how she explained our presence to the kids, but I have absolutely no doubt that she did. They were well aware of what was going on and why we were there.

"They were lovely kids and they treated us with the utmost respect. They knew us by our names in the end.

"I'd go as far as to say that she was a decent woman. But having said that, what she did, God almighty, it was horrific by any standards. But to talk to her and deal with her, she came across as good."

By the time Linda and Charlotte went on trial in October 2006,

BEAST OF BALTINGLASS: Larry Murphy had stalked, beaten and raped his traumatised victim before being disturbed by passing hunters. Just over a decade later, he emerged from jail (inset) and free to roam our streets

JAILED FOR LIFE: Brian Kearney who was found guilty of the horrific 2006 killing of his 37 year old wife Siobhan (below left)

SAD END: The family home in Knocknashee in Dublin's Goatstown

LIMERICK MAYHEM: Owen Treacy (above left), who was the key witness in the gangland trial for the murder of Kieran Keane (above right) for which five Limerick crims were jailed for life

LEFT: Brothers Eddie (left) and Kieran Ryan pictured at at their home in Kileely, Limerick after their 'abduction'

SCUM: Keith Wilson, who was jailed for life for the murder of Finglas thug Daniel Gaynor (above right) who was shot dead at Barnamore Crescent (right) in August 2010

KILLER LOOK: Joe O'Reilly, who was convicted of the callous murder of wife Rachel (pictured above on their wedding day) at their home in Naul, Co Dublin in 2004, a crime that shocked the nation

VICTORY FOR JUSTICE: Rachel O'Reilly's family, the Callalys, walk out of court arm in arm to celebrate killer Joe's conviction in July 2007

NEIGHBOUR FROM HELL: Wayne O'Donoghue is led away to begin his sentence for the 2005 killing of young schoolboy Robert Holohan (inset) Right: Parents Mark and Majella try to comfort devastated daughter Emma at Robert's funeral at Midleton, Co Cork

SCISSOR SISTERS: Linda and Charlotte Mulhall from Tallaght who killed and chopped up the body of Farah Swaleh Noor, whose torso was later found in the canal at Ballybough Bridge, close to Croke Park
Right: Their mother Kathleen Mulhall,was later jailed for aiding and abetting the concealment of a crime

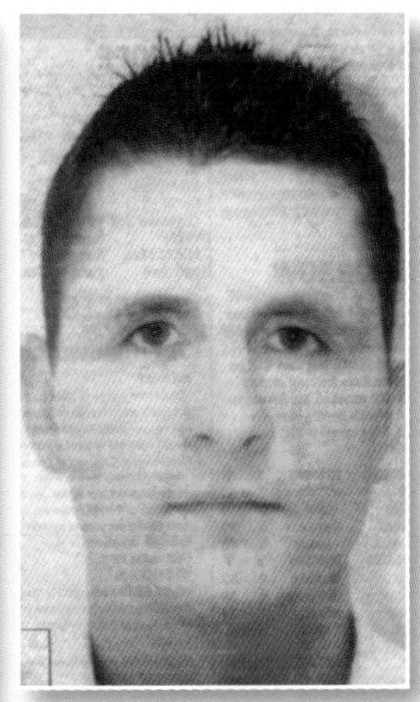

GANG BOSS: (clockwise from above) 'Fat' Freddie Thompson; dead criminal Darren 'The Fonz' Geoghegan and convicted hitman Craig White, who was jailed for the 2005 killing of Noel Roche

BROTHERS IN ARMS: Drug dealers John and Noel Roche who were shot dead in separate attacks, and (right) Gavin Byrne from Crumlin who was shot dead in Dublin's Firhouse estate along with his partner in crime, Darren Geoghegan

BEAUTY AND THE BEAST: Swiss national Manuela Riedo (23) was raped and murdered by sex monster Gerald Barry (left) during her 2007 visit to Galway. Her devastated parents Arlette and Hans Peter Riedo spoke of their constant pain after Barry's court conviction

Below: The exact spot where the body of Manuela was found under the tree

LIGHTS, CAMERA, ACTION: Eamonn Lillis was convicted of killing wife Celine Cawley at their plush Dublin home (inset) in 2008. He had initially claimed that he had disturbed a violent robber at the house but in 2010 Lillis was convicted of manslaughter and jailed for almost seven years

COLD CASE: Vera McGrath was jailed for her part in the murder of her husband Bernard Brian McGrath (below); while at bottom of page, her partner in crime Colin Pinder (below left)is pictured alongside his former lover Veronica McGrath who helped crack the brutal crime and bring the two killers to justice

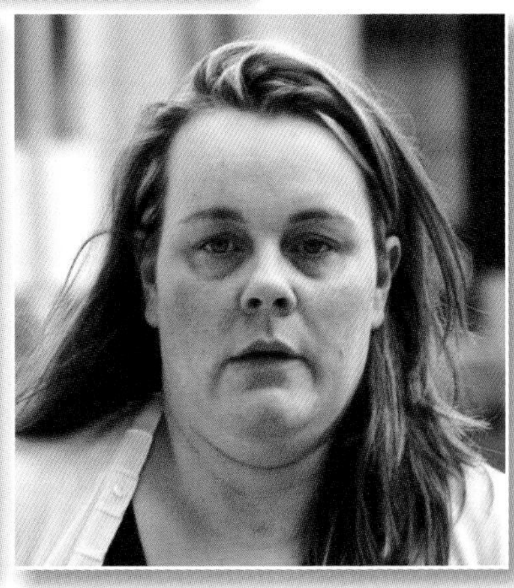

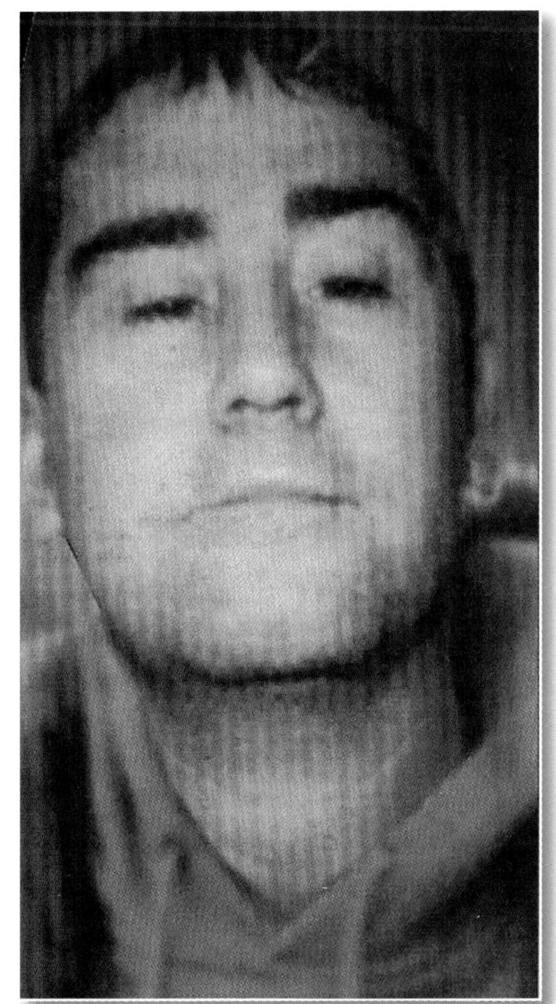

BLOODY END: Michael Taylor Jnr (31) of Summerhill who was convicted of killing Paul Kelly (below), who was shot dead on April 6, 2007 at the door to an apartment block on Dublin's northside

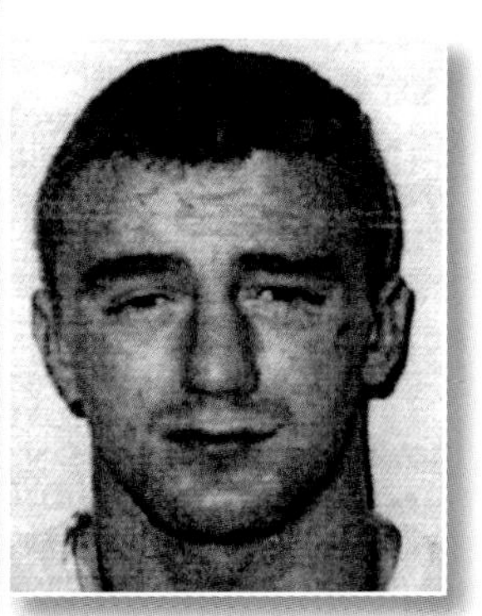

BANGED UP: Perverted Christy Griffin

SHOT: Michael Taylor Snr (right), from Summerhill Cottages in Dublin's inner city who was shot in his holiday home in Donabate on June 6, 2011. He was shot by two men and he died of his injuries the next day

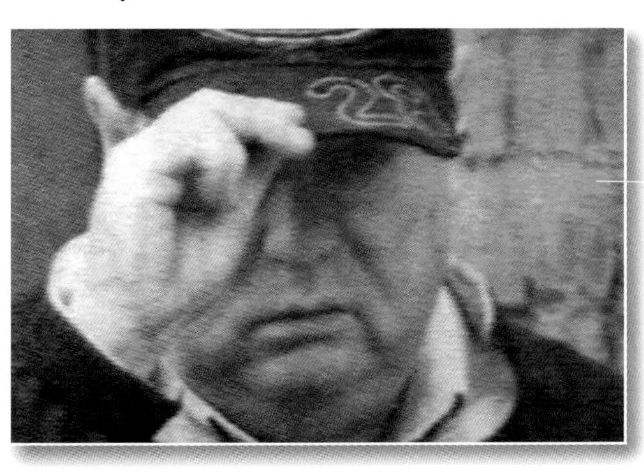

BLACK WIDOW: Catherine Nevin who was jailed for the killing of her husband (inset) Tom Nevin and (left), the couple appeared happy as they posed outisde their pub, Jack Whites in Co Wicklow, in1996

their dad John had committed suicide and their brothers James and John had several brushes with the law.

It later emerged that James Mulhall took advantage of breaks in Linda and Charlotte Mulhall's trial to go to the International Financial Services Centre (IFSC) in Dublin's docklands and steal from prostitutes.

He was ultimately identified after detectives recognised him in court from mugshots of those suspected of stealing from the prostitute, which had been circulated around Dublin Garda stations, and jailed for five years in 2008.

By the time the murder trial started, the sisters' mother Kathleen had fled to London and could not be contacted by gardai.

The central plank of evidence against the sisters was their statements to gardai.

In her voluntary statement, Linda admitted that she was sitting on Charlotte's lap in the sitting room listening to a CD when Noor, who had been earlier making threatening gestures at their mother Kathleen, came in and put his arm around her waist.

Kathleen asked: "What the f**k are you doing?" and Linda recalled: "Farah kept saying, 'You're so like your mammy.'"

Linda said that Charlotte was telling Noor to get his hands off her when her sister picked up a Stanley knife and cut his throat.

Noor then staggered out of the room into the bedroom and hit his head on a bunk bed.

At this stage, Linda picked up a hammer and continued to batter him over the head with it while Charlotte stabbed him.

Linda recalled: "I picked up a hammer and hit him on the head loads of times, a good few times and Charlotte stabbed him."

She said Noor was dragged into the bathroom by the legs where "me and Charlotte chopped him up. It was Charlotte's idea."

Linda said she was in the shower area while her sister sat on a toilet seat as they set about their truly horrifying task.

Charlotte started sawing his legs off with a bread knife, but she quickly became tired.

Linda then used a claw-hammer to hit his legs several times, and both sisters put towels over his legs to stop the blood gushing out.

Linda said they took turns doing both gruesome jobs, and it took a number of hours for them to cut up the body in the bathroom.

She later remembered: "The smell — it wouldn't go away. I think about it every night."

Apart from cutting off his legs, the women cut off his head and his penis — neither of which have ever been found.

In her interviews with gardai, Charlotte said she could not remember who cut off Noor's penis and head.

During their trial, a garda told the court that Charlotte recalled her mother had told her: "Just cut him up."

As the panicked women stood around screaming, Kathleen Mulhall said: "Get him out."

In her statement, Charlotte initially denied that she had been at the flat at the time of the killing and said she and Linda had been drinking "all over town" that night from 10pm until 5 or 6am the next morning, when she came home to find her mother Kathleen covered in blood.

She said at first she thought her mother had been assaulted by Noor but then her mother said she had killed him with a hammer and by cutting his throat, before chopping up his body.

Asked about her sister's earlier statements to gardai in which Linda had confessed to the killing she said: "I just think Linda is mad for saying things she didn't do."

Asked why she had said this, she said: "Because we promised my ma we would say we did it." She said her mother had threatened to kill herself if she went to prison.

However, later in the interview when she was asked what happened, Charlotte said: "Everything that Linda said."

Charlotte broke down in tears in front of gardai and agreed with detectives that she loved her sister and had wanted to protect her.

She said Noor had made threats to her mother, adding: "She just told me he kept saying to her 'I'm going to kill you before the year is up.'"

She said her sister and her mother had been drinking and taking ecstasy at the flat. "Farah didn't want to take 'E' but my mother crushed up an 'E' and put it in his drink and said he'll be on the same buzz as us," she recalled.

Charlotte said Noor then started saying things to Linda and would not let her go.

She said: "It was something like we're two creatures or something similar."

Everyone was arguing and she said: "Ma kept saying to me and Linda please just kill him for me then she got the hammer and the knife and she gave them to me and Linda, but he wouldn't let Linda go and I cut him on the neck."

Charlotte had indicated to officers the side of her neck in the interview and told them: "It was just a blade or a knife, I don't remember."

She said Linda was hitting him with a hammer.

Asked who stabbed Noor, she replied: "I don't remember everything that happened," but she said she remembered stabbing him in the neck and having a knife.

After he died she said the three women did not know what to do with him. She couldn't remember if they had rung anyone or not and she told gardai: "Me mammy said 'Just cut him up.'"

She said she and her sister then cut him up in the bathroom, adding: "I just remember cutting; I cut him up with the knife". She said she used a kitchen knife while her sister had a hammer.

Once their grim work was done, they placed the body parts into a sports bag and bin bags.

They then made several trips to the nearby Royal Canal where they disposed of various parts of Noor's mutilated body in the shadow of Croke Park.

The sisters put Noor's head in a bag and took a bus to Tallaght, where they buried it in Tymon Park.

A few days later Linda returned to the park, dug up the head and placed it in her son's schoolbag before taking it to a nearby field. She finally kissed it before burying it again.

But 10 days after the brutal killing, parts of Noor's body, including his arm, leg, torso and thigh, were discovered in the Royal Canal just a stone's throw from where he met his grisly end — and the Garda investigation began.

In the aftermath of the sisters' case, Det Supt Mangan admitted: "For a variety of reasons this was a particularly difficult incident to resolve, right from establishing the identity of the victim through to bringing a prosecution before the courts."

While Linda and Charlotte had to face justice and a high-profile trial, their mother fled to England.

In February 2008, detectives eventually tracked Kathleen Mulhall down at a location in west London where she had been living with a new African lover — a convicted rapist from Sierra Leone.

In England, she had dyed her hair blonde and was going by the name Kathy Ward, which is her maiden name.

After meeting the officers, Kathleen Mulhall then voluntarily agreed to come back to Ireland to face the music.

Within 24 hours she had been brought before Dublin District Court and on February 13, 2008, Kathleen was charged with obstructing the arrest or prosecution of a person who has committed a murder.

Kathleen spent over a year on remand at Mountjoy Women's Prison, also known as the Dochas Centre, where her notorious daughters are also serving their sentences.

Despite having the occasional heated row, Kathleen enjoyed a close relationship with her daughters, who continued to attract huge media coverage.

In August 2008, the *Evening Herald* published a photo of Charlotte Mulhall holding a 12-inch kitchen knife to the throat of a male inmate while behind bars.

The photo showed her holding a long blade to the neck of Mountjoy inmate Denis Gibney, who was celebrating his birthday with a cake.

The publication of the photo caused huge controversy as well as major embarrassment for the Irish Prison Service, who ordered that Charlotte be transferred to Limerick Prison for a number of months as punishment.

Prison Service boss Brian Purcell said in a statement: "Evidence we have to date indicates that the photograph was taken over a year ago in the prison kitchen, where the prisoner worked, and the knife itself was a kitchen knife.

"Security issues are of paramount importance to the Prison Service. We already have a rolling programme of security reviews within the prison system, and in this context we will shortly be conducting a full security audit of the Dochas Centre.

"As part of the new package of security measures currently being rolled out across the prison system, new airport-style security measures, which include walk-through detectors and X-ray scanners are scheduled to go live in the Dochas Centre, commencing on 4 September.

"Everyone coming into the prison — prisoners, visitors and staff — will have to pass through the new measures, and all handbags, briefcases, clothing, etc, will be subject to screening."

The prison officer suspected of taking the infamous photo was later jailed for smuggling drugs into Mountjoy Prison.

On February 17, 2009, a clearly distraught Kathleen Mulhall pleaded guilty to cleaning up the murder scene at Richmond Cottages in Ballybough.

Kathleen had originally been charged with nine offences relating to Noor's death, but the Director of Public Prosecutions accepted a guilty plea in relation to one charge.

A tearful Kathleen said only one word — guilty — and her voice could barely be heard in the busy courtroom.

On May 5, 2009, Kathleen was sentenced to five years in prison for impeding the investigation into the notorious crime.

The experienced judge who passed sentence was the same one who sentenced her daughters, Mr Justice Paul Carney.

Addressing Kathleen, Mr Justice Carney said: "It was the most grotesque case of killing that has occurred in my professional lifetime."

Dressed in a brown pinstripe jacket and a pink shirt, Kathleen showed no reaction when the judge said that mitigating factors in her case included her "lifetime of being subjected to abuse and violence at the hands of her family and the men with whom she had relationships".

Among those who abused Kathleen was her husband John, who gardai believe played a role in the murder and that his suicide by hanging in the Phoenix Park was as a result of guilt he felt about it.

In an interview with RTE which was broadcast in May 2011, retired garda Dan Kenna spoke about his suspicions that John Mulhall Snr played a bigger role in the shocking saga.

He said: "I always believed that John Mulhall had a more active role at some stage. We're not sure what his role was there, but we know there was contact between the father, his wife, and two children."

Mr Kenna explained: "The taking of his own life would not be in keeping with the character of John Mulhall, and we're unsure why that man took his own life.

"We have accounts of him beating his wife Kathleen and his children during their early years. Perhaps the burden of it was too much for him to bear, and the only way for him to deal with it was to take his own life.

"We will never establish for certain what went on in Richmond Cottages the day Farah was killed.

"We are happy we have established the murder scene, we had ample evidence to support the fact he was murdered in that flat.

"We only have the accounts of Linda Mulhall and Charlotte Mulhall to tell us what happened.

"We have a separate account from Kathleen Mulhall that distances her from the killing.

"We will never know how they could dismember a body in that area and leave so little evidence.

"You have to remember this was a living human being who had just been killed, whose body was still warm.

"For him to be cut up in the manner he was into so many separate pieces in such a small area and to leave no trace of that part of the crime poses the question of whether he was actually dismembered at the same location."

In July 2009, Kathleen was questioned in jail over claims that her murdered partner had killed teenager Raonaid Murray.

Mulhall previously gave statements to gardai in which she

alleged her lover had told her twice he was the man who killed Raonaid on a street near her home in Glenageary.

A team of cold-case detectives met Mulhall to go over the contents of those statements but no major breakthrough could be made in the Raonaid case and Noor has now been ruled out as a suspect.

But what is not in doubt is that Noor was an extremely dangerous person.

Noor's real name was Sheilila Said Salim. He arrived in Ireland in December 1996 and sought refugee status. His initial application was turned down in 1997.

He appealed, claiming he was from war-torn Mogadishu, that his family had all been killed and that his life would be in peril if he returned. It was all lies. He was born and brought up in Kenya by his Somali parents.

He was granted asylum status here in 1999. Two years before that, he raped and impregnated a mentally disabled Chinese girl who was only 16. She later gave birth to a son.

In April 1998 he met and seduced another 16-year-old girl from Tallaght. She, too, was soon pregnant. She moved in with Noor after their son's birth.

She said that at first he behaved well but later began drinking and taking drugs and regularly beat and raped her. When drunk he often burned himself on the arms and forehead with lit cigarettes. He always carried knives.

Of eight criminal charges that Noor faced for disorder and assault, one involved a sexual assault in which a knife was found at the scene by gardai. He was convicted on three occasions but did not serve time in jail.

He was a drifter staying in various flats and houses in various locations around Dublin and in two locations in Cork city.

In late October 2011, Kathleen was released from prison and she lives a lonely life in a northside bedsit, living for Saturdays when she travels to the Dochas Centre to visit her two killer daughters who she abandoned in the aftermath of Noor's murder.

In July 2012, Kathleen did an extraordinary interview with

former Justice Minister Nora Owen on TV3 where she said she would kill Farah Swaleh Noor herself if she met him now.

She also said she longs for the time when she can be reunited with her daughters.

"If he was standing in front of me, I'd f***ing kill him myself," Kathleen told TV3's Midweek, though she added she did not really mean she would kill him.

In her first television interview since being released from jail, she said: "I dream about myself and my two girls living together someday, all together, but I'm 58 and I'm not that well all the time, so who knows.

"I don't know what the future holds. Nothing has ever worked out for me so, I just live one day at a time. I don't plan anything."

Kathleen said she did not know "what came over" her daughters when they savagely killed Noor.

She said: "I'm still trying to get my head around what happened. They're not violent girls, they were never violent."

She added: "Sometimes I find myself wandering back up to Richmond Cottages (in Ballybough), that's where Farah and I lived, and I stop and think, 'Oh God, he's not there, he's not coming back.' He didn't deserve to die in that way. No-one did."

Kathleen explained that she had no sympathy for Noor's Kenyan family as she never knew he had a wife.

In fact Noor had married Husna Said when she was 17. They had three children together, Somoe, Mohamed and Zuleh.

Somoe was aged 17 when she died shortly after learning of her father's gruesome death.

Her mother Husna later explained that Somoe "got a shock over her father's death". Husna added: "She was 17 years old, the first born. When she heard the news, she got a fever and lost her memory.

"She then fell into a coma for two days and died. She was in high school. She lost consciousness and never woke up. I miss her so much because she was a beautiful person. Sometimes I feel like killing myself. Sometimes I want to commit suicide because I have nothing left in this world."

Noor had left his family over ten years before he was murdered when he came to Ireland in December 1996 and had two children with different women while he was here.

In her TV interview, Kathleen said she would never have destroyed her life by "going off with" Noor if she had known he was already married, adding: "He was no little angel."

She said she has been abused verbally on the street and assaulted once since her release. She cried as she recalled how leaving her two daughters in Mountjoy Prison's Dochas Centre was the hardest moment of her life.

"It was just like my life had ended...they are my children, I'm their mum. It was hard walking away and leaving them there," she said.

CHAPTER 8

Gang Implosion

The bitter Crumlin-Drimnagh feud – a gang war between opposing Dublin drugs mobs – had its bloodiest 48 hours in November 2005.

In that space of that time, three criminals were shot dead in brutal gangland executions as the feud, which had started almost five years earlier, spiralled into its most dangerous phase.

What made these three gun murders stick in the general public's minds is that they happened in affluent, middle-class areas of the capital – far away from the mean south inner-city streets where the warfare began after former drug-dealing comrades accused each other of informing to gardai about the gang's operations.

The 48-hour cycle of killing started on the night of November 13, 2005, when drug dealers Darren 'Fonzy' Geoghegan (26) and Gavin Byrne (30) were shot dead as they sat in a car in a housing estate in leafy Firhouse, south Dublin.

Geoghegan and Byrne were senior members of a gang led by the now-exiled gang boss 'Fat' Freddie Thompson, whose mob were in a bitter turf war with an equally psychotic crew led by jailed murderer Brian 'King Ratt' Rattigan.

However gardai are certain that Rattigan's crew had nothing to do with the gruesome double murder and instead are convinced that it was the result of an internal 'Fat' Freddie gang dispute over money.

The murdered duo – who had grown up together and entered a life of crime together in Crumlin – died as they sat together in the front of the car when a gunman or gunmen unleashed a volley of shots into the vehicle from two Glock pistols.

No-one has ever been charged but it has since emerged that the double murder was planned by Freddie Thompson's gang for months and they enlisted two separate criminal groupings from Bray, Co Wicklow and Hillsborough, Co Down for "major logistical support" for the slaying.

A senior Garda source said: "These gangs sourced vehicles used in the double murder and were also involved in destroying the cars after it was carried out.

"The fact that the Thompson gang used two different criminal organisations for this hit shows how well it was planned and how organised it was. The two groupings would not have known each other and may not even have been told what they were providing logistical support for until the last minute."

Gardai have been investigating the murders for the past seven years and have been working closely with the PSNI to try and track down the vicious killers. The PSNI have arrested three criminals in the North on suspicion of conspiracy to murder while gardai have made five arrests.

The focus of the PSNI investigation is to track down who sourced a silver BMW connected to the murders. This vehicle was caught on CCTV crossing the border just days before the killings. While the PSNI have been working on that aspect of the investigation, gardai have also arrested five men they believe took part in the crime.

One of these is a major-league crime lord from Bray, Co Wicklow, who has links with a Black VW Golf car used in the killings. This vehicle was found burnt out in Bray shortly after the murder. The Bray crime lord has been based in Spain since 2008 and for years had very close connections to the 'Fat' Freddie Thompson gang.

Geoghegan and Byrne were in an English-registered silver Lexus car in the middle-class Carrigwood estate in Firhouse. Detectives believe the pair were in the area after a meeting was arranged with one of their own gang members.

Despite the arrests and the massive investigation, the case has now run cold. An inquest into the deaths was held in May 2012, in which Detective Inspector John Walsh said there was insufficient evidence to prepare a file for the Director of Public Prosecutions and the case remained open.

Just two days after the double murder and with gang tensions at almost record levels in Dublin, a key member of the Brian Rattigan gang was murdered after he left a concert in the venue formerly known as the Point Depot and now The O2.

Noel Roche (27) was a serious criminal with convictions for assault, firearms and traffic offences. He was also a key target of 'Fat' Freddie Thompson's organisation because he was a senior player in the Rattigan faction.

In a separate unsolved Crumlin-Drimnagh feud murder, Noel's younger brother John (24) – also a gang member – was shot dead outside his apartment in Kilmainham, south Dublin, just eight months before Noel was targeted. The 'Fat' Freddie Thompson mob are the chief suspects for this slaying, which occurred on the night of March 9, 2005.

Sources say that the death of his younger brother had a devastating effect on Noel Roche but he continued his life of organised crime and had planned to exact revenge for the shooting. However a night in November 2005 would be Noel's last on this earth and it ultimately sparked legal history, with gardai being able to secure the first murder conviction over a fatality linked to the Crumlin-Drimnagh feud.

Noel Roche was shot dead at point-blank range as he sat in the passenger seat of a Ford Mondeo on posh Clontarf Road at around 10.30pm on Tuesday, November 15, 2005. He never stood a chance – shot three times in the face and chest.

Pathologist Dr Michael Curtis carried out the post-mortem – and concluded that a bullet entered Roche's left cheek and exited the back of his skull. Two bullets entered his chest. There was no doubt that this was the work of a professional hitman.

Earlier that night Roche had attended a Phil Collins concert at the Point Depot with his girlfriend, aunt and uncle. Also present was Roche's driver – small-time criminal Eddie Rice from Kilworth Road in Drimnagh. While Roche listened to Phil Collins, Rice stood guard, making sure that everything was OK and that Roche was "being looked after".

At around 9.30pm, Roche and his girlfriend went out to the lobby bar for a drink. While he was there, Noel Roche saw somebody linked to his bitter gangland rivals. It is not known whether that person was a rival gang member or an associate of the Thompson gang, but he was concerned enough to leave the concert early for his own safety. He sent his girlfriend to tell his aunt and uncle that he had to go and dispatched Eddie Rice to get the car and pull up out front so they could safely leave the area.

Roche and Rice were unaware that they had been seen early in the night and were probably under surveillance while at the concert. A person inside the venue is known to have made a phone call to Paddy Doyle. Doyle, from north inner-city Dublin, was a notorious hitman linked to a number of murders in the Crumlin-Drimnagh feud.

Roche's aunt Margaret McMahon later told gardai she and her husband had gone to see Phil Collins at the Point Depot with Mr Roche and his girlfriend. Mrs McMahon said that at around 9.30pm Mr Roche went to out to the bar in the lobby for a drink with his girlfriend. His girlfriend returned to the main arena and said Mr Roche had to leave.

An eyewitness who later came forward to gardai was waiting outside the venue in his car to collect his parents from the gig. He noticed a Fiat Punto parked in front of his car. He said the driver was a large man who looked too big for the vehicle. He also saw a man on the pavement who was smoking, wearing a hoodie and going back and forth to the Fiat Punto. Its registration was 04 TS 839. The man then noticed a Ford Mondeo pull up.

The witness later told officers that a 5'9" man with black hair, in his 30s and on a mobile phone jumped into the Ford Mondeo, which took off at speed in the direction of Clontarf. The Fiat did a U-turn in the middle of the road and followed the Ford Mondeo.

The witness drove his parents to the north side of the city and later heard on the radio that there had been a shooting. Out of curiosity he drove to the scene as reported on the news and saw the same Ford Mondeo he had observed outside the Point. He said he knew by the tinted windows, the colour of the car and its lack of hub caps that it was the same vehicle.

After leaving the concert, Rice drove Roche and his girlfriend to her apartment in Coolock, north Dublin, before they decided to go back into the city centre. They had no idea they were still being followed by notorious gunman Paddy Doyle and his driver, Craig White, a then 19-year-old up-and-coming criminal from O'Devaney Gardens in north inner-city Dublin.

At around 10.25pm, their Peugeot 307 began to rev up behind Rice's Mondeo, attempting to ram it off the Clontarf Road. The Peugeot had been stolen from a property in Blessington, Co Wicklow, some weeks earlier.

As Roche and Rice approached the well-known Yacht Bar, White managed to swerve across their path, leaving Paddy Doyle and Noel Roche side by side in the middle of the road. Doyle wasted no time and fired four shots from his 9mm Glock handgun into the passenger side of the car. Roche was killed instantly. Doyle and White then drove their car at speed to nearby Furry Park Road in Killester, dumped it and fled on foot.

Driver Eddie Rice was uninjured in the shooting but was covered in his pal's blood when he fled the scene, abandoning his Mondeo car. He began knocking on doors, trying to wake householders. Several people answered their doors in their nightclothes, only to quickly shut them when they saw a man covered in blood screaming frantically at them.

Rice managed to make it into a back garden and escaped, leading to a major manhunt as people speculated whether he had been shot dead as well. A third murder in the space of just 48 hours – all linked to the same feud – caused genuine public concern.

The following day the *Evening Herald* newspaper published photographs of Roche as he sat in the passenger seat of the Ford Mondeo car – his face disfigured from the horrendous gun injuries he had received. Shortly before the *Herald* hit the streets on

Wednesday, November 16, 2005, the now deceased DJ Gerry Ryan – who ironically died from a cocaine overdose in April 2010 – spoke of his shock that a gangland feud fuelled by two warring cocaine gangs was leading to such violence in the middle-class Dublin suburb where he lived.

On his extremely popular radio show on 2fm, Ryan opened with an interview with RTE's crime correspondent Paul Reynolds in which he expressed his shock that such crimes were now spilling out of more working-class areas into middle-class suburbs like Clontarf and Firhouse, where three murders had happened in the space of just 48 hours.

"The shooting that took place is what is another chapter in this tit-for-tat gangland return-fire shootings. It happened on the Clontarf Road last night . . . two or three minutes away from my own hall door," Mr Ryan pointed out.

Later in the interview, the DJ explained: "My understanding from talking to one eyewitness last night was that the man looked like his head had been decapitated. There was a huge and immediate response in Clontarf.

"I could hear the sirens. I was making supper at the time and getting ready to go to bed. The area was ablaze with blue lights. They [the gardai] instantaneously responded. We had the helicopter surveilling the area, there were unmarked cars around the area . . . . I was thinking this morning as I listened to this story unfold, 'How could they [the gardai] have prevented this?'

"Unless they got intelligence from within these two gangs it would be virtually impossible."

By the time that Gerry Ryan spoke about the shocking assassination that had happened on his doorstep, the investigation team, led by detectives from Clontarf and Raheny Garda Stations, had already gathered vital information and important intelligence that Paddy Doyle and Craig White were involved in the murder.

Of crucial importance was that Doyle and White had abandoned the getaway car without setting it on fire, which meant that very valuable forensic information could be obtained from items left in it. These included a brown paper bag containing a balaclava, a gun, a tea towel and a pair of gloves found in the rear driver side of the Peugeot. Two gloves were also discovered on the Furry Park Road and a container of petrol was found in the footwell of the abandoned Peugeot.

Meanwhile, gardai sealed off the scene of the shooting minutes after Roche was shot. A short time later, the dead man's mother, Caroline – who had lost her second son in eight months due to gangland feuding – arrived at the scene.

While there, the distressed woman named Paddy Doyle as the man who had shot her son. She also claimed that he had shot Noel Roche from the back of a motorbike – which investigations later established was incorrect. But gardai believe she was certainly right about the first part.

Earlier, Garda Colm Mac Donnacha was one of the first officers on the scene and he later recalled that the Ford Mondeo was abandoned in the middle of the road with the driver's door lying open. The lights were on and the key was in the ignition, but the engine was not running. He looked through the driver's door and saw a male slumped backwards in the front passenger seat. He also noticed four bullet holes in the passenger window. There was no sign of the driver.

He said the male passenger showed no signs of life. Garda Mac Donnacha moved to the passenger side of the vehicle and saw four 9mm bullet casings on the ground. He noticed that the windows of the car were tinted, so he could not see the passenger from outside the vehicle.

Detective Jeremiah Maloney carried out a technical examination of the blue Peugeot 307 which was abandoned on Furry Park Road not long after Roche was shot. Inside the brown paper bag found in the rear of the driver's foot well he found the Glock semi-automatic pistol, balaclava, tea towel and gloves. The car was examined for fingerprints and firearm residue.

Detective Sergeant Shane Henry, a ballistics expert, examined the Glock pistol. He later told Craig White's murder trial that the serial number had been ground off and this had damaged the weapon, causing it to jam after a certain number of shots were fired.

From an examination of bullets and cartridge cases found at the scene of Roche's shooting, Detective Sergeant Henry believed they were fired from the pistol he had been asked to examine.

He said the cartridge cases were found on the ground outside the Ford Mondeo in which Mr Roche died and their position indicated that the person who fired the weapon was within a short range of the car.

As specialist officers were dealing with the crime scene, other gardai conducted door-to-door enquiries at Clontarf Road. An elderly lady who lived there told them she heard shots but tried to persuade herself it was fireworks until a man came to her door shouting for her to ring gardai and an ambulance. She said he told her that there had been a very bad car accident. It would later emerge that this man was Eddie Rice.

Another witness who lived on Furry Park Road told gardai that at around 10.30pm she went out to the front of her house and heard a car driving past at high speed. It pulled up across the road and she saw two men in their 20s running away from it. She described the men as of average height and build. She then noted the registration of the car and rang gardai.

Garda Philippa Cantwell was in a patrol car which responded to a call about a shooting. She noticed the driver was missing from the abandoned vehicle containing the fatally injured Roche, and was possibly injured himself. Garda Cantwell searched the streets around the scene of the shooting but did not find the driver.

Eddie Rice eventually turned up after 40 hours on the run and handed himself in to gardai. He was arrested by detectives in Raheny for withholding information. Gardai had urged Rice to turn himself in as it was feared he had been kidnapped by the gang who ambushed his pal. Gardai also believed that he could have been wounded in the attack and might have needed urgent medical treatment. However, as it turned out, he had not been hit.

During two days of questioning – which involved gardai going to Dublin District Court for a time extension – Rice refused to utter a word and also refused to enter the Witness Protection Programme. This meant he was freed from Raheny Garda Station, no help to what was now a massive investigation.

But gardai did not need Rice's assistance. Before he was even arrested, officers had made another significant discovery.

Sergeant Gerard McCarthy was part of a search team which examined an area surrounding Furry Park Road the day after the murder. He found two blue sports gloves in a garden and on the footpath. By December 5, 2005 – three weeks after the murder, gardai were certain that they had enough evidence to arrest White and Doyle for Roche's murder.

But Doyle had fled to Spain's 'Costa Del Crime' – and he was murdered there in February 2008.

White was still in Dublin, and he was picked up by detectives at his girlfriend's home in Cabra, north Dublin, on the night of December 5. In fact, White had very close links to a dangerous gang of young criminals from the Cabra area who would be involved in the shocking murder of innocent mother-of-two Baiba Saulite less than a year later. No-one has ever been charged.

He was brought to Raheny Garda Station, where he was questioned for a number of days. He refused to co-operate with detectives except to give details of a false alibi and deny any involvement in the brutal slaying. However, White did agree to hand over forensic samples from his body and, when these were compared with items found at the crime scene, a damning case would be built against him.

Detective Ray Kane had found three fingerprints and one thumbprint on the paper bag found in the getaway car. Two days after the murder, he had searched the Gardai's Automated Fingerprint Identification System (AFIS) using a thumbprint from the bag – and White come up as a result. After the suspect's arrest, Detective Kane compared the fingerprints on the bag to prints taken from him at Raheny Garda Station.

At the murder trial almost four years later, the garda said he had no doubt White had handled the bag. Detective Kane had taken fingerprints from White on December 5, 2005 and later matched White's right thumb, left little finger, right forefinger and right middle finger to the marks he took from the paper bag.

However, no prints at all were found on the pistol inside it, and White's prints were not found anywhere in or on the Peugeot 307, other than on the bag. A large number of unidentified prints were also found in the car. After White had given swabs for DNA testing, tests by Michael Burrington of the Forensic Science Laboratory showed that a DNA profile extracted from the handle of the bag containing the murder weapon was a match.

This was a massive breakthrough, helped by the fact that partial DNA profiles had been extracted from the gloves found on Furry Park Road which also matched White's.

After being questioned for two days, Craig White was released without charge. Sources say that many on the investigation team felt that there was not enough evidence to convict the young criminal. In April 2006, a file was submitted to the Director of Public Prosecutions but it decided that no charges should be brought at that stage.

However, as White continued with his life of crime, the investigation team did not give up on this case and lots of attention was given to this dangerous young man.

By the summer of 2006, he must have felt he was untouchable – popular with the ladies and respected by serious players in the underworld, he seemed to be going places in gangland. Sources believe he played a role in the horrific murder of Latvian woman Baiba Saulite in November 2006.

Gardai have always suspected that Baiba's murder was ordered by her ex-husband – feared Lebanese criminal Hassan Hassan (42), who left Ireland for Syria in March 2010 after serving jail sentences for kidnapping his sons and running a stolen-car racket. Hassan was arrested twice in relation to his wife's murder. It was while Hassan was in prison that he approached members of Limerick's evil McCarthy-Dundon gang to organise the murder.

Gardai have always worked on the theory that the McCarthy-Dundons passed on the contract to murder Baiba to the Dublin gang controlled by Martin 'Marlo' Hyland, himself executed less than a month after the Latvian mum was murdered. In turn, Hyland used some of the younger criminals in his organisation to carry out surveillance and ultimately murder the tragic 28-year-old. These younger criminals were made up of a vicious Cabra-based crew of which White was an important member.

As the months turned into years, Craig White must have thought he would never be charged with the murder of Noel Roche. His partner in crime for that ruthless hit – Paddy Doyle from Portland Row in Dublin's north inner city – had settled into a life of serious crime in Spain. Gardai did not have enough evidence to get a European Arrest Warrant to extradite him back to Ireland but they did plan to arrest him if he set foot back in Dublin.

Doyle continued to be involved in drugs trafficking and in Spain he mixed and socialised with some of the most serious players in international crime – traffickers from Turkey, Russia and the Balkans. Paddy Doyle was in the 'A' league of European crime.

But his life came to an abrupt end on the afternoon of February 4, 2008 – murdered on the outskirts of Estepona, near Marbella in Spain. He was travelling with convicted criminal Gary Hutch and gang boss 'Fat' Freddie Thompson.

The three men were in a high-powered BMW 4x4 in the Cancelada district when gunmen opened fire from another car. Four shots were pumped into the front windscreen and another into the front passenger door, before the driver, Gary Hutch, a nephew of Gerry 'The Monk' Hutch, lost control of the vehicle. The BMW smashed into a lamp post and Doyle, who was a front-seat passenger, attempted to run away.

But the gunman began firing again and Doyle was struck twice in the head at point-blank range. The attack took place at the Bel-Air apartment complex shortly after lunchtime and eyewitnesses said the gunmen made their escape in another BMW 4x4.

Back in Dublin, White was understood to be upset about the murder – but continued to run into constant trouble with the law, mostly for minor offences.

Just nine days after Doyle was murdered, White was arrested in Mountjoy Prison by Detective Inspector Paul Scott – where he was serving a short sentence for minor offences. It was February 13, 2008, and unknown to White, gardai had built other strands to the forensic case against the gangland criminal for the killing of Noel Roche.

The investigation team – then led by Detective Superintendent Michael Byrne – had found out from a number of informants that White had boasted about his involvement in the murder to a number of other people.

By using mobile technology, gardai were able to establish that White was in Ratoath, Co Meath, 35 minutes after the killing – a fact that blew his alibi completely out of the water.

After his arrest, more forensic material was obtained from White. He was released without charge and returned to Mountjoy. The situation was now very serious for the gangster, although he was not charged with the murder until exactly seven months later, on September 13, 2008.

Tensions in the Crumlin-Drimnagh feud were at a very high level in the autumn of that year, with almost daily gun and pipe bomb attacks – and it is perhaps for this reason that there was no official notification to the media that a man was to be charged with murder in Dublin District Court that sunny Saturday morning. This is highly unusual – almost unprecedented, in fact – especially with a murder case being cracked after almost four years and with convictions in gangland cases so rare at that time.

But Garda management were probably right to be cautious. Just a couple of hours after White was charged, small-time drug-dealer Christy Barry (28) was shot dead in a bookies in Killester – a murder linked to the ongoing Crumlin-Drimnagh gang warfare. Liam Bolger, of Homelawn Gardens, Tallaght, is currently serving a life sentence for this murder – also successfully prosecuted by gardai from Clontarf and Raheny.

Less than four hours before this outrage, Craig White appeared at Dublin District Court for just a few minutes to hear evidence of his arrest, charge and caution. Detective Sergeant Enda Mulryan said White had nothing to say when the charge was put to him. He was remanded in custody and convicted 11 months later – a well-respected figure within the serious gangster community in the prison system.

White was found guilty of murder on July 29, 2009, after a jury of seven men and five women took little over half an hour to convict him – surely influenced by the damning forensic evidence. It later emerged that the extremely concerned jury had requested that their daily roll call be conducted in private each morning rather than in open court because of the gangland nature of the case.

CHAPTER 9

Savage Murder Of Student

The savage rape and murder of a teenage foreign student in Galway in October 2007 caused huge panic in the city and across the entire west of Ireland.

Pretty Manuela Riedo (17) had arrived in Ireland just three days before she was brutalised in the worst way imaginable.

The tragic student from Bern in Switzerland suffered a terrible ordeal. She was attacked on a shortcut into Galway city from the suburb of Renmore along waste ground beside a railway line near Lough Atalia – known locally as 'The Line'.

Before her murder, Manuela had been making the most of her planned two-week break in Ireland with a group of 43 pupils and two teachers. She was attending intensive language classes during the day and enjoying the unique atmosphere of Galway's bars in her last evenings alive. It was October 8, 2007, and Manuela was on the way from her host family's home on the outskirts of the city to the King's Head pub in the city centre when she was set upon.

Her host, Martin Tierney, had warned her not to take this shortcut. It was badly lit and people walking along the path had been victims of petty crime – but what Manuela endured was horrific. She was grabbed from behind by an armlock and strangled by a vicious attacker, who also raped her. The teenager was also beaten around the head and had cuts around her vagina as well as a gaping wound to her groin.

A patch of skin two inches by three had been removed from Manuela's groin area. Markings around the wound indicated that she had been cut with a knife. The State pathologist, Marie Cassidy, later concluded that death was due to asphyxiation. Her attacker had pressed down so hard on the student's neck that the thin gold chain she wore with two small gold crosses left a lasting imprint on her skin. It was a truly savage crime.

Her pals in the King's Head pub were oblivious to Manuela's ordeal. Her friend Azaria Maurer sent her a text just before 9pm. "Where are you – are you not coming to the King's Head?" it read. The next morning, Azaria noticed her friend was not in class. She tried to phone her mobile, but the automated voice told her the phone was no longer in use. When Manuela's battered body was discovered the next morning by local artist Sam Beardon, it was naked from the waist down but partially covered by her coat, which was secured by a rock.

Mr Beardon first noticed a rucksack in the middle of a clump of bushes on the muddy path, then a purse nearby – and then the tragic teenager's body.

He later recalled: "I saw a bag, a bright flowery backpack like a student would carry. I thought, 'My God, what's that doing there, maybe someone was robbed and they discarded the bag here after they went through it?'

"Then I squeezed through some bushes and I found a Durex on the ground, ripped open. I thought, 'That's funny, teenagers these days'. I saw something pale and I think I knew straight away. It was the colour of skin."

The barbaric crime shocked the entire country and got huge media coverage in Manuela's native country. Two days after the murder, gardai warned young women not to go out alone in Galway city. Superintendent Tom Curley, now a chief superintendent in charge of policing Co Mayo, led the investigation into the horrific crime. In its aftermath he warned: "When out socialising at night, students should travel in pairs. Don't go to isolated areas or areas which are unlit or there is no CCTV."

By this stage, one of the biggest murder hunts in Galway's history was underway, with 50 gardai working around the clock exclusively on the case. But already officers had made a crucial breakthrough. After the crime scene was sealed off, Detective Shane Curran noticed a used condom snagged on a nearby bush, and this proved to be a very important development.

Gardai also made the important discovery that Manuela's mobile phone and camera had been stolen.

A source close to the investigation told this author that in the days after the murder, local gardai spent a lot of time "compiling an overview of suspects which included anyone from the locality with a history of violence or of sexual offences".

A vicious local thug called Gerald Barry, then aged 27, was one of the first names to appear on the "overview", according to the source – and the real significance of this emerged when gardai studied hours of CCTV.

They spent the week after Manuela's murder examining files on suspects for previous physical and sexual assaults in Galway city and surrounding towns. This included using VICLAS, the Violent Crime Linkage Analysis System, a computer system developed by the Royal Canadian Mounted Police in the early 1990s to compare different crimes for similarities.

Barry was well known to officers in the city: he had 60 previous convictions and had served a five-year jail sentence for violent disorder in an incident during which a man died, as well as a two-year sentence for an aggravated burglary in which a pensioner lost the sight in his remaining good eye.

In the first incident, tragic Colm Phelan (26) from Tipperary was enjoying a stag night when he and his friends were set upon by the crazed gang of teenagers. Colm died after being struck over the head by a bottle in Eyre Square in the centre of Galway. Colm's mother, Marie, later said: "My son went down to Galway for a stag night out and Ger Barry decided that he was going to attack him, so he did, and four other chaps with him. Three of them were sentenced to two years and Gerald got five years, of which I'd say he served about two-and-a-half to three years and he was back out on the streets."

The year before Manuela's murder, Barry was also jailed for six months for sexually assaulting his ex-partner. He was on bail at the time of murder in relation to that assault as well as being the chief suspect in the rape of a French student on August 16, 2007 – an offence which he was later convicted of.

In relation to the assault on his ex-partner, the woman, who cannot be named to protect the identity of the couple's son, told gardai she was asleep at about 5am on a terrifying August morning in 2007, when Barry climbed onto the front-door canopy and got in through her bedroom window upstairs. He jumped on top of her in the bed and started strangling her with both hands.

"He had his hands around my neck trying to choke me while I was lying on the bed. He was really violent," the woman said.

The noise, she added, woke her then two-year-old son, whom she held in her arms as she tried to escape.

Barry pushed her so hard her head hit off their son's head. Barry kept pushing her and the child back into the bedroom but she managed to run downstairs and open the front door, screaming. Barry then left the house – but not before waving his fist in her face while threatening to kill her and their young son.

She said Barry had been demanding money from her when he first came into the bedroom. He told her gardai had taken his car and he wanted money to get it back. "My main concern was to get my son to safety before he [Barry] did anything else," the woman added.

Unfortunately, when Barry was brought before a special sitting of Galway District Court in August 2007 for the assault on the woman and the child, the woman told a visiting judge presiding over the courts holiday period that she was not afraid of Barry and, as a result, he was granted bail. Less than 18 hours later, he committed a savage rape against a terrified French woman.

Like Manuela, the French student was walking home alone in an isolated part of the outskirts of Galway city when Barry attacked her. "Do what I want and I won't kill you. I just want to shag you," he whispered in her ear after he crept up behind her, grabbed her by the hair and held a knife to her throat.

He dragged his victim to St James's GAA pitch on Walter Macken Road. He threatened again and again to kill her if she turned to look at him. She told him she was a virgin and pleaded with him to let her go. But he had no intention of releasing her. Instead, he began to pull at her clothes and touch her body.

She told gardai: "He asked me if I liked it. I said, 'No'. He said, 'You will like it.'" He forced her to her knees and then raped her anally. She felt like it would never end. He continued to threaten her, saying: "I know where you are living. If you go to the police I will kill you." As he raped the traumatised woman, he continued to talk to her. "You're a nice girl . . . I have the power over you."

Halfway through the ordeal, he told his victim that if she gave him oral sex one more time he would let her go. But afterwards, he refused. Instead, he ordered her to take off her clothes and anally raped her twice more. After the final rape, he noticed that the woman was cut. This pleased him. "Hey," he exclaimed. "You are bleeding, great."

He eventually let her go, all the while threatening to kill her if she told anyone. The 21-year-old was studying at NUI Galway and working part-time as a waitress at the time. She had been on the way home after enjoying a night out with friends listening to traditional music when her path crossed Barry's. She stumbled home, showered and tried to sleep. The next day, she went to hospital but had to write down on a piece of paper that she was raped. She was too traumatised to speak the words.

The memory of Barry still fresh in her mind, the student was initially too terrified to speak to gardai but eventually gave them a full statement.

"He is not a human or a man. He is a liar, a rapist and a murderer. I beg you not to let him out because he will do it again," she told detectives. "How can he sleep at night, be living, breathing, walking, laughing and listening to music?"

Just two months after this French woman was raped, Barry struck again.

Officers were aware of the earlier rape but they did not have enough evidence to charge him. However they knew enough about Barry to know he was a person of major interest in the Manuela murder case.

Gardai had identified their suspect but hard evidence was needed to progress the investigation. CCTV footage from Mainguard Street in Galway showed Barry walking down the street wearing a red jacket and carrying a plastic bag. The significance of this is that it placed him relatively near the location where Manuela's body was found.

When questioned by gardai after his arrest, Barry denied it was him in the image. "No, no, he's taller than me. I've never owned a red jacket or a baseball cap," he told detectives. But witnesses, including Barry's brother Kevin, had told officers that Barry was wearing those clothes on the night.

Ten long days after Manuela was murdered, gardai arrested Barry. Almost 20 officers were involved in the arrest because they knew about the brute's extremely violent nature and expected him to resist. When they searched his apartment at Rahoon in Galway on the day of the arrest, Detective Shane Curran found Manuela's Olympus digital camera in his bedroom between the mattress and the bed.

Asked about this by detectives, Barry claimed: "It's the first time I've ever seen one of those cameras, the only ones I've seen are disposable. I've never seen a camera in the bedroom."

The investigation got another breakthrough when officers retrieved the Sony Ericsson mobile phone Barry stole from Manuela. The evil predator had sold it to an associate for €30 and this man sold it on to another man, who passed it on to his brother. When this last man put his SIM card into it, he noticed there were a lot of messages written in a foreign language. He then gave the phone to his father, who handed it to gardai as he was aware of their appeal over a missing mobile in the murder hunt.

By now gardai knew that they almost had their man, but groundbreaking mobile-phone and DNA technology would make their case against Barry watertight.

During questioning, Barry insisted that he was nowhere near the crime scene at Lough Atalia on the night of October 8, 2007. But officers enlisted the services of Meteor phone engineers, who carried out detailed analysis of Barry's mobile. The scrutiny showed that calls from his phone were routed through a cell at the Lough

Atalia and Renmore areas on the night in question. This damning evidence contradicted what Barry had told gardai: "I haven't been there for years. I haven't been anywhere up there drinking for years."

The detailed analysis showed he had made a call routed through a specific cell in the Lough Atalia area at 7.19pm, around the time Manuela was walking in the area.

After his arrest, gardai took DNA swabs from Barry and used a helicopter to rush the samples taken from him and the condom discarded at the murder scene to the forensic laboratory in Dublin. There, Dr Maureen Smith carried out tests and discovered the condom's contents matched the DNA profile of Barry. The chances a person unrelated to Barry having the same profile were one in a thousand million – he was well and truly snared.

Detective Seamus Burke asked: "Can you explain how your DNA and that of the girl were on the condom?"

Barry replied: "I can't answer that question because I don't know."

When pressed further, he said: "I haven't worn a condom in the last five years so I don't know how my DNA is in the condom."

Barry's ridiculous denials were of no use to him now and he was charged with Manuela's murder, at Galway District Court on the morning of October 19, 2007. The beast snarled and lashed out when a large crowd of locals jeered, jostled and heckled him as he was led out of the courthouse, to be remanded in Castlerea Prison in Co Roscommon.

On the same day, around 500 mourners led by Manuela's grief-stricken parents Hans-Peter and Arlette gathered for her dignified and emotional funeral near her home in Hinterkappelen, a suburb of the Swiss capital, Bern.

True to form, Barry pleaded not guilty to murdering Manuela when he went on trial at the Central Criminal Court in March 2009, but admitted stealing her camera and phone. In court, Arlette and Hans-Peter sat and quietly listened to all the evidence every day, holding hands at particularly difficult moments. Hans-Peter broke down in tears as he heard details of the horrific injuries his daughter suffered.

In the witness box, Barry claimed that she died by accident shortly after the pair had consensual sex. He said he met the teenager when she asked him for the time outside a shop in Renmore on the night she died. He engaged her in conversation and, on hearing that she was going into the city centre to meet friends, walked with her to show her a short cut through the wasteland, he claimed. Barry brazenly claimed that Manuela agreed to have sex with him, but tried to leave shortly afterwards.

"I sat up behind her and grabbed her from behind. I told her not to go, to stay with me for a while longer," he said. He added that he made a joke but noticed that something was wrong when she did not respond. Barry said he "panicked" and dragged Manuela's body into the bushes and then took her phone and camera.

The jury did not believe his story and took just two hours and 38 minutes to find him guilty of murder, on March 22, 2009, following a seven-day trial. He was given the mandatory life sentence.

Before this was handed down, it took Detective Superintendent PJ Durkin 20 minutes to read his list of previous convictions, which included the fatal attack on Colm Phelan, when Barry was a teenager.

Imposing sentence on the sick killer, Mr Justice Barry White said he was in complete agreement with the verdict, which he said would be shared by all right-thinking people. He also expressed his sympathies to Manuela's parents and added he hoped they can "find it in their hearts to forgive the Irish nation". The judge acknowledged that Barry came from a dysfunctional family, but he told him: "You clearly have a substantial criminal record that involves violent behaviour."

In fact the contrast between Manuela's innocent and loving upbringing and Barry's childhood could not be more different. He was one of nine children and he witnessed severe abuse in his childhood, when he was regularly beaten. His mother suffered from mental-health problems and Gerald Barry spent much of his childhood in institutional care. But his horrible childhood cannot be used as an excuse for his sickening crimes.

After the verdict, Hans-Peter Riedo said it had been difficult for his family to sit through the trial and listen to all the lies said about his daughter, their only child. He explained: "The defence said many things about Manuela and they were all lies. I want everyone to know that about her. We are happy with the outcome, but at the end of the day, Manuela has died. But Ireland is a safer place and your children are safer now. I don't want to say what I think about him. He is the devil. We hope and pray that no, he won't be released. It will be better for all people."

Thankfully Hans-Peter's wishes about Barry never being freed look very likely to come true.

On July 24, 2009, the evil monster was given two further life sentences for the rape of the young French student, an attack that happened just seven weeks before he murdered Manuela. Imposing the maximum sentence, Mr Justice Paul Carney said: "From the accused's previous records, I believe he is a person who has the propensity to kill and rape and is highly likely to do so again." The judge added that there was no "tunnel of hope" for Barry and that "the scourge of drugs made some people mindless, wholly irrational and evil".

Barry is now expected to spend many decades languishing in the Midlands Prison in Portlaoise, where sources say that he is "despised" by other inmates and has been attacked on a number of occasions. The senior garda who led the investigations against the twisted predator summed up his feelings about Barry being jailed for life in very simple terms.

"Galway is a safer place for everyone with the imprisonment of Gerald Barry," said Superintendent Tom Curley.

Speaking on RTE's Liveline show after Barry's conviction, Marie Phelan, whose son Colm had died violently in 1996 following an attack by a group including the 16-year-old Barry, said she was "absolutely horrified" to discover he had got out of jail and been able to kill again.

Mrs Phelan had gone on Liveline in August 2000 to say how important rehabilitation is for people like Barry, and her emotional plea at that time was replayed for listeners nine years later – after his horrific murder of Manuela.

"He [Colm] was just the unlucky one that didn't come home to us. My family is devastated," Marie Phelan said in that earlier interview. "It just doesn't help these youngsters when they go to jail. They need something else. They need somewhere to be educated, to learn how to love and live and behave when they are out. I hope no family will ever go through what we have gone through, getting that phone call in the middle of the night to say our son was dead. No mum or dad, brother or sister wants to hear that."

When she spoke to presenter Joe Duffy this time, Mrs Phelan recalled how gardai had contacted her family to tell them that the man charged with Manuela Riedo's murder was the same one who had attacked their son 13 years earlier. "I was absolutely horrified that he got out and was able to kill someone else and that there was no help to rehabilitate him back into society," she said. "They are coming out of prison worse people than going in."

The Riedo murder trial had brought back all the trauma surrounding Colm's death, she added.

"Colm would be 39 now. No-one can walk the streets any more. Everybody is afraid to go out at night," she pointed out. "It's gone so bad that I'll just have to appeal again to people to stop and think about what they are doing. If they could come into someone's homes and see the devastating effect that all this has on the families of the dead people they murder.

Mrs Phelan continued: "I wouldn't want to see him [Barry] walking the streets again unless he has received a lot of therapy. He is a very sick man who needs lots of help."

Meanwhile, the memory of the innocent teenager that Barry so brutally violated and murdered lives on in the hearts of many people in Ireland and Switzerland.

The fourth anniversary of Manuela's death in October 2011 was marked by a flight of balloons against the backdrop of the Burren in Galway city. Her parents, Arlette and Hans-Peter, were among several hundred people at the ceremony before the annual fundraising concert, A Night for Manuela, in Salthill. A bagpiper played a lament before a countdown to the balloons release. The Mayor of Galway, Hildegarde Naughton, and a number of gardai who worked on the investigation into the murder were there.

"Today we are happy to be back," the Riedos said, adding they felt their daughter's presence at the memorial event at Ladies Beach.

A day earlier, they spent two hours at the location near Renmore where their daughter's body was found. Every time they returned to Galway they recognised more familiar faces, the couple added.

A total of 60 students from Ms Riedo's Swiss college, Ecole Professionale in Fribourg, travelled to Galway for the anniversary. They were joined by 60 Galway students as a mark of solidarity between the two communities.

The fundraising concert, initiated by Galway man Shane Lennon and friends in 2008, has raised around €100,000 to date. The money is being used to provide education and support programmes for young people, in conjunction with the Galway Rape Crisis Centre.

But, despite all the sympathy and goodwill shown to them by Irish people, Manuela's parents understandably feel very bitter towards our country's justice system.

In an interview in July, 2011, her dad, Hans-Peter, said Barry should never have been freed and hearing that he already had a string of convictions was almost impossible to take.

"That was almost as difficult as the news of her death," he stated. "When we realised what he had done before, how many crimes he had committed, and that someone like that was set free. It was well known how dangerous he is and they just let him go. And on October 8, when he killed Manuela, he should have been in custody for the French girl he raped. That's what hurts the most. It was the mistake of the Irish justice system. If not for them, Manuela would still be alive today and we would have our old, beautiful life back."

CHAPTER 10

Bond Girl's Horror Ending

It would end up being the murder trial that had everything – sex, infidelity, deceit, characters from the highest echelons of Irish society and a former glamorous Bond girl who was a loving mother-of-one when she was battered to death at her plush home.

The upmarket north Dublin suburb of Howth had never had a crime quite like this before. The morning of Monday, December 15, 2008, was a particularly crisp, frosty and sunny winter's day but as the sun shone the scene that greeted gardai – at Rowan Hill, a €3 million detached modern mansion on posh Windgate Road which had spectacular views from Howth Head – was extremely grim. The emergency services had been contacted at 10.04am that day when TV-advert producer Eamonn Lillis made a frantic 999 call answered by Kevin Moran of Tara Street Fire Station.

During the 10-minute phone call Lillis gasped for breath as he explained how he and his wife had been assaulted. There were lengthy pauses in which Lillis was heard explaining that he was unable to detect any breathing from his wife, despite attempts to resuscitate her.

"My wife has been attacked," he told the emergency services, going on to give the address of the family home in Howth. When gardai and paramedics got to the property, Lillis's wife, Celine

Cawley, was dead and she had severe head injuries. Paramedic Stephen O'Reilly from Kilbarrack Fire station later explained: "The temperature of her body appeared colder than what it should be for the time she was exposed on the deck.

"The patient seemed to be cold to touch," he added.

Mr O'Reilly made his important assertion based on the time the emergency call came through and the time paramedics arrived at the scene. Lillis told gardai that a burglar had attacked his wife and fled through the back garden of his home, so officers drafted in the help of the air-support unit after he gave a detailed account of what this man was supposed to look like.

Later that day at a press conference, then head of the Garda Press Office Superintendent John Gilligan told reporters: "We know, from what we've heard, the man ran down the back garden of the house, out on to a laneway and may have made his way in any direction after that but in particular the Windgate Road-Carrickbrack Road area."

But even at this stage, the investigation into the murder of Celine Cawley was heading in a very different direction.

Detective Inspector Angela Willis – now a superintendent based in Cavan – led the investigation. She first met Lillis in his kitchen as his wife was being stretchered away. When the highly skilled and ambitious female detective asked him for his consent to have the house forensically and technically examined, he replied: "Whatever it takes. I just want him caught."

Celine was pronounced dead at Beaumont Hospital and just a few hours after that her husband was in Howth Garda Station giving a statement to detectives. Not long after he was brought to the Garda station he asked to go to the toilet. When a garda asked Lillis not to wash his hands, he said he had already washed them at home. Lillis also agreed to hand over the clothes he was wearing – a grey hooded sweatshirt, grey T-shirt and green combat trousers – so they could be forensically tested.

In a statement to Detective Sergeant Enda Mulryan, which the detective wrote while Lillis spoke, he explained how he got up at 6.30am that morning and did sit-ups. At 6.50am he made tea and brought a cup to his wife of 17 years, whom he had met in Kinsale in September 1990. He explained that she had a bad cold and so he had slept in the upstairs bedroom while she slept downstairs. He said they watched television in her bedroom until 7.40am, when he went for a shower.

He then brought their teenage daughter, Georgia, to school in his black Mercedes jeep, unlocking the electric gates to leave. He said he met an old college friend and spoke about getting ready for Christmas. "I told her I put the lights up last night and they blew," he said.

He went to the nearby Summit Stores shop in Howth, bought *The Irish Times* newspaper and drove home, unlocking the gate again. "The dogs ran up to the car. I decided to take them for a walk," he said of his three pets, a Rhodesian Ridgeback, a Cocker Spaniel and Molly, an old Newfoundland. "I went into the wash-room to get their leads and hooked up Sam and Harry."

He said the door wasn't locked and he did not see his wife at this stage. They were not going to work until later and had a meeting scheduled for 2pm with their pension provider.

"Celine started the company. I came in about two years later as a partner," Lillis explained of Toytown Films.

He described the route he took with the dogs and said he saw nobody on his walk. On returning he let the dogs off their leads and put some rubbish in the bin before going through the wash-room into the kitchen.

"That's when I saw him on top of Celine," he said. "I don't know what he was doing. He was at her top."

Lillis continued. "I charged out the door, roaring."

He said the assailant sprang to his feet and swung at him with a brick. "I slipped," he explained, giving details of the scuffle. "Then he legged it." Lillis said he didn't know how he hurt his fingers, one of which had to be bandaged by ambulance staff earlier as the nail had come away from the nail bed.

"He was wearing a ski mask, definitely not a home-made bala-clava ," he said, describing the man's gloves as "nylon" and his jeans as "dark blue".

"I saw his mouth. He was definitely a white male. I saw him run away after he floored me," he went on, suggesting that the man he was describing had run towards the back of the garden, where there was a six-feet-high fence. "We had fencing put up to the back after the last burglary," he explained.

Lillis said that he went numb when he saw no movement from his wife but managed to dial 999.

"When I pressed on her, she exhaled," he said, explaining that he performed CPR on the instructions of the person who took the emergency call. "We've no enemies," he said. "I can only assume it was a burglar." He said he suspected the man was wearing a balaclava because they might have known him. He named the man they suspected of burgling the house before. "It was never proven," he said, adding that they had received a warning that this person was back in the area carrying out more burglaries.

Dr Haroon Khan attended Lillis at the Garda station on the evening of his wife's death.

"I noted he had multiple visible scratch marks on his right forehead and the left side of his face," he said. "His left ring finger and right little finger were also injured and there were abrasions on his kneecaps. The injuries were consistent with his being in a struggle with another person."

The following day, at Howth Garda Station, Lillis went into even more detail with his second statement. "I don't know if it was my imagination, but I think she opened her eyes. I don't know," he said, referring to when he was trying to check his wife's pulse. He now said that this had been after he passed out due to the intruder hitting him. He didn't know for how long he passed out.

Lillis also gave more detail about the 5'11" attacker's clothes, saying there was a cream or white stripe around the balaclava and the sleeves of the bomber jacket were a different colour and material to the rest of it.

"It was a bit like a garda's jacket," he said.

The investigation into Celine Cawley's murder involved a number of key components – apart from taking and comparing witness statements, gardai also trawled CCTV and carried out a detailed forensic examination of the house in which Lillis and his family lived. Lillis had told officers he visited the Summit Stores in Howth to buy a newspaper on that fateful morning and the investigation team made a key breakthrough when they obtained CCTV footage from the shop.

The footage, which was in colour, was unusually clear and it showed Lillis wearing jeans, a dark sweater and dark runners with a white strip along the sole at 8.35am, after he had dropped daughter Georgia to school. Significantly, when gardai arrived at his home less than two hours later, Lillis was wearing different clothes. Of course this meant that he had changed – and the big question had to be why.

Over the coming days gardai canvassed hundreds of witnesses, including a woman who spoke to Lillis when he dropped his daughter off at school. Both his demeanour and appearance were "normal" and he had no scratches on his face at that stage.

But Emma O'Byrne, commercials producer for Toytown Films, the company which Celine Cawley owned and Lillis worked for, told gardai that when Lillis rang her in the office later that morning, he sounded "quite distressed". Of major importance was a statement made to gardai by Pauline Frasier, a neighbour of the unhappy couple, who told officers how a high-pitched scream woke her up at 9.30am that Monday.

"It was like a shriek," she said, adding that it sounded like a woman. "It struck me as very odd. It's a very quiet road. About 30 seconds later it happened again. It was very unusual. I thought there was someone in trouble. It would have struck you as though something had happened to somebody."

The fact that a woman had screamed at 9.30am in the locality, combined with the fact that Celine's body was colder than it should have been when paramedics arrived at the scene, showed that Lillis had lied about what time his wife had been assaulted. The thorough forensic examination of the large property took days to complete, but after it was finished gardai had enough evidence to get their man.

While they combed the house for evidence, Lillis stayed with Celine's brother Chris Cawley as he was obviously not able to stay at his own home while detailed investigations took place. During his time with his brother-in-law, Lillis was prescribed Valium and sleeping tablets. Three days after his sister's death, Chris Cawley had a conversation with Lillis about an article in the *Evening Herald* newspaper which said a brick had been used as the alleged murder weapon. Lillis told Mr Cawley it was a "non-story, ridiculous because everybody knows the brick was found. Sure, didn't I hold the brick in my own hand."

During this week, Lillis was in constant voluntary contact with gardai as officers continued to search his home. In the days after the fatal incident, Eamonn Lillis made a number of calls to Detective Sergeant Gary Kelly. He wanted to know when he could return to his home, and how the investigation was going. He called the detective five times over two days.

A crucial development happened three days after Celine Cawley was killed – gardai searching Rowan Hill found a black suitcase in the attic which contained Lillis's bloodstained clothes in a refuse bag. The discovery was made by Detective Colm McDonagh. These were the clothes Lillis had been wearing when he was caught on camera buying a paper at the Summit on December 15. They were not the clothes he had given gardai and claimed to have been wearing when his wife sustained her injuries.

A black jumper showed heavy contact staining on the front, there were bloodstains on the front of a pair of jeans and light spots of blood on a pair of blue-and-white striped boxer shorts.

The right of a pair of black outdoor gloves was heavily bloodstained and both of a pair of blue latex gloves were heavily stained. All the items came up positive for Celine Cawley's DNA after testing by forensic scientist Dr Linda Williams.

Dr Hilary Clarke of the Forensic Science Laboratory, who carried out tests on items of clothing and swabs taken from the scene, said the blood and DNA samples had matched Eamonn Lillis and Celine Cawley and no third-party DNA had been found. She also found that blood and tissue imbedded in the clasp of a watch found on Eamonn Lillis's bedside table matched that of Celine Cawley.

When Lillis went on trial for his wife's murder, Detective Alan Curry told of finding the watch. "Initially it appeared perfect," he said. "However when I picked it up I noticed the face had been smeared. The links in the wrist strap had blood-like staining and the clasp had blood-like staining and tissue embedded in it."

A pair of black runner boots found in a wardrobe at the house showed airborne blood staining, meaning the boots had been "nearby when blood matching Celine Cawley's travelled through the air", according to testimony from Dr Clarke. Drops of blood on a cream roller blind had come from Ms Cawley, while swabs from the bathroom sink had matched both hers and Lillis's. Swabs from blood spatters on the outside wall at the patio had also matched Celine Cawley.

What was particularly damning for Lillis is that gardai also found seven pieces of heavily bloodstained paper towels and tissue in the refuse bag in the suitcase in the attic. The paper towels tested positive for the dead woman's DNA while the tissue was her husband's – tests would later show that the diluted nature of the blood indicated that there had been an effort to clean it up.

Detectives had earlier seized a bloodstained cobblestone from the patio of the death house. It had been beside Ms Cawley's head as she lay unconscious in a pool of blood.

Mobile-phone technology also played a major role in the investigation: gardai got information that Lillis was having a passionate affair with his masseuse – a woman called Jean Treacy, originally from Nenagh in Co Tipperary. Investigations established that Lillis and his mistress exchanged more than 200 text messages and almost 90 calls in the fortnight before his wife's death.

Detective Patrick Connell examined two mobile phones and three SIM cards belonging to Lillis and two phones containing SIM cards belonging to Jean Treacy. The first recovered contact between them was on November 2, 2008, and phone traffic between them increased after that.

Detective Connell recovered a number of deleted messages from one of Lillis's phones, including this one sent by Ms Treacy at 10.57pm on the night before the death:

"Transporter 3 good. Love Jason Statham. You staying at home tomorrow? K going into the office for part of morning so can meet you somewhere. Miss u so much x." Less than three minutes later she sent another message: "No pressure though ok baby x."

Another two minutes later she wrote: "Well as usual I'll have to play it by ear but will contact you as soon as possible in the morning. Night my love. I love you infinitely. Sleep well x."

On the morning of December 15, the day of Ms Cawley s death, Jean Treacy texted at 10.26: "Everything ok?" And another at 11.14am: "Getting a bit worried now babe x." By then Celine Cawley had been pronounced dead in Beaumont Hospital.

The following day she sent a couple of texts designed to reassure Lillis: "Don't want you to think I'm abandoning you but also to create a distance between them, till things have calmed down (for both our sakes)." It hadn't been an easy decision to make, she wrote. "You know that I miss you and will be thinking of you every step of the way," she added.

In another text, she told him she still felt the exact same and would see him at the funeral. But by the time of the funeral Eamonn Lillis would be in custody, charged with his wife's murder.

Mobile-phone investigations established that the pair exchanged 86 text messages, four multimedia messages and 18 calls during November 2008. In the first 16 days of December they exchanged 212 text messages and 88 calls.

While searching the house, gardai also found a note on Lillis's bedside locker. It read: "She will get that wedding dress. She will marry Keith in June. She will send out the invites in January. You will never be with her properly. The only way to be with her is to live here. Think of the positives in the relationship. You will never take her to France. She will never share your bed. You are running out of time!!!"

This was clearly a reference to Jean Treacy and her plans to marry her long-term partner Keith Fahey – an event that did not happen until August 2012. And before gardai were ever able to trawl through mobile-phone evidence, Detective Sergeant Gary Kelly interviewed Ms Treacy for a number of hours during which she admitted having an affair with Lillis for the past 10 weeks.

The first time they'd had sex was in Lillis's home, Ms Treacy explained. The affair began 16 months after Lillis began attending the Howth Haven beauty salon, where Treacy provided his weekly deep-tissue massage. They hit it off in mid-October 2008.

When first questioned by the gardai, she described Lillis as "refined and gentle", a bit of a dreamer and "somebody who wouldn't hurt a fly". She told officers how Celine Cawley introduced her husband to her, referring him for massage. She gave Lillis deep-tissue massage, mainly on his back.

In her statement, which she elaborated on during Lillis's dramatic murder trial in January, 2010, she recalled that he spoke about his dogs quite a lot and she told him she'd love to see a picture of them.

Jean Treacy told the court that one evening after a treatment, she sat in the front seat of his car with the door open to look at a picture of the dogs on his iPod.

"The rapport between us was quite different that day. I noticed his hands were really nice for a man's," she said. "The next week he was mentioning that the muscles on the front of his shoulders were quite sore. I turned him around. Normally people close their eyes when you turn them around, but he didn't."

Instead, explained Ms Treacy, Lillis had stared and smiled at her.

"He was permanently staring at me, to the point where I was almost uncomfortable . . . I asked him what he was thinking. He just kept staring and smiling."

She said he then asked her what she was thinking. "I put his fingers on my pulse and my pulse was racing and I said, 'That's what I'm thinking,' and I walked out of the room."

Ms Treacy later said they were both somewhat embarrassed. She revealed that there was a different atmosphere between them the following week, about eight weeks before Ms Cawley's death. That was when their affair began.

She said she met him almost every day and they communicated by phone and text, with him buying her a second phone to be used only for him. As far as she knew Ms Cawley didn't know of the affair. She and Lillis didn't initially discuss his marriage. She said she would not have known that they were having problems until he told her about four or five weeks before his wife's death that he was unhappy.

"As an outsider you wouldn't know anything was wrong between them. They looked very good together," she stated.

Lillis's mistress explained that she saw him most Mondays, with him texting her in the morning first. However, she said she heard nothing from him on the Monday morning that Ms Cawley was killed. "I had sent a text at 10 asking him to bring the ML jeep, not from a seedy or sordid point of view, but just that when we were sitting in the front seat it would be more comfortable," she said. "The windows are tinted so you're not looking over your shoulder."

She said she was concerned when she didn't hear back from her lover. Ms Treacy pointed out that it wasn't until 6.40pm, when her then boss phoned her, that she heard what happened. She sent Lillis a text offering her support.

"At that point I was 100 per cent convinced there had been a burglary," she explained. "I got a text back saying, 'It gives me great strength that you re thinking of me.'"

There were no calls between them but more messages including one in which he mentioned his "horrifying day, a day from hell".

Ms Treacy suggested he give his daughter a hug and tell her everything would be OK. She finally suggested they drop all contact for a while.

As gardai built up a full picture of Lillis's infidelity, studied the forensic evidence and compared witness and CCTV evidence, they were also furnished with a post-mortem report on Celine Cawley by deputy State pathologist Michael Curtis.

He found that she died after suffering three blows to the head – two of which were dealt as she lay unconscious and face down on the ground. The first blow knocked her down; the following two blows were inflicted as she lay motionless. Scratches on her face were consistent with it being in contact with the ground while the blows were delivered to the back of her head, Dr Curtis said.

The pathologist revealed that Ms Cawley's life could have been saved if medical assistance had been given in time.

The post-mortem also found that Ms Cawley suffered from an enlarged heart and was obese, which complicated her breathing and blood loss as she lay on the ground. Dr Curtis gave the principal cause of death as blunt-force trauma to the head with haemorrhage and postural asphyxia, and with contributory factors of obesity and enlargement of the heart. Dr Curtis said he was told the victim, who was 5'10" tall, had been found face down.

"Such a posture, particularly in an obese woman, would have

splintered her diaphragm, dangerously impairing her ability to breathe," he explained.

Dr Curtis said she bled profusely from her skull, so her heart would have been seriously deprived of blood flow and oxygen. Her enlarged heart would have increased the demand for both blood and oxygen, he said. Dr Curtis said Ms Cawley's head was blood-soaked when he conducted his post-mortem.

With all the different strands of the investigation coming together, gardai felt that they had enough evidence to arrest Eamonn Lillis for his wife's murder – just five days after she was killed.

Early on the morning of Saturday, December 20, a number of gardai called to the Howth home of Celine's brother Chris Cawley, where Lillis was staying.

"Eamonn Lillis was in a bedroom alone. I went to the room and woke him up," Detective Sergeant Gary Kelly later explained. "At 6.55am I arrested him for the murder of his wife, Celine Cawley."

Lillis was taken to Clontarf Garda Station. Throughout that day and into the following morning he was interviewed by a number of gardai. He was asked about the state of his marriage and whether he had killed his wife.

"Our relationship on a professional and personal level was very, very good. She was a tower of strength for me, I didn't kill her. I swear before God I couldn't do it," he insisted.

Later, he was asked about a local beauty salon, the Howth Haven, which he attended regularly for a massage. Who looked after him there?

"Jean, I can't remember."

"Jean Treacy?" he was asked.

"Yes," he admitted, when confronted with the fact that Ms Treacy had already talked to officers.

After further questioning Lillis admitted that he had been having an affair. He put it down to a "mid-life crisis" and insisted it had absolutely nothing to do with what had happened to his slain wife. As experienced gardai tried to coax the details of her death out of him, Lillis consistently denied any involvement. Teams of detectives worked on him in pairs all that day.

Detective Pat Flood told Lillis: "Nobody said you are a nasty bloke. Everybody said you are a decent, soft bloke. There has to be an explanation. Let that soft bloke come out."

Detective Paul Donoghue told Lillis that the gardai's inquiries had discovered that Celine Cawley was "a dominant person, slightly on the bullying side". There was also a suggestion that Lillis was "a second citizen" in the relationship.

Detective Donoghue also told Lillis that they had heard that she would regularly shout at him to "Come here, do this." That he was "a lapdog".

He put it to Lillis: "It's obvious a terrible tragedy happened. Everything points to the fact you had a row with Celine. It is within all of us to crack up and get very, very angry. Your head flipped that morning. From what I heard about you, everybody, to the last person, is saying you are a nice guy, a gentle, caring person. You have to face up to what happened."

However Detective Donoghue also took a tougher approach when he suggested to Lillis that his report of an intruder was "a cock-and-bull story" as he had never heard of burglars stashing material in attics to retrieve at a later stage. He claimed Lillis's explanation that the scratches on his face were due to a gesture of love by his wife was "preposterous".

"You're in the film industry. You should be better at making up things up," remarked the detective at one stage, adding that Lillis's description of the intruder "wouldn't hack it in Postman Pat".

Lillis still would not admit any guilt under questioning, even when confronted with CCTV and forensic evidence, but a day after his arrest the DPP decided he should be charged with murder. He was remanded in custody the following day after a brief court appearance.

Eamonn Lillis then spent three weeks on remand in Cloverhill Prison in west Dublin before finally being released on bail. After his release he attempted to re-ignite his relationship with Jean Treacy and kept gardai informed of his advances – which were, in fact, a breach of his bail conditions.

Lillis's murder trial started in January 2010 and was one of the most dramatic and controversial in recent times, especially when gardai screened star witness Jean Treacy from waiting press photographers. This led to a media feeding frenzy to get the first photo of the woman having an affair with a murder accused.

The case was notable for the huge media it attracted. During the trial Lillis changed the account he gave investigating gardai of the tragic events that had led to Celine Cawley's death.

On the opening day, his lawyer, Brendan Grehan SC, revealed on his behalf that there had been no burglar in the house that day.

When Lillis finally took the stand he gave an account of a violent row with his wife over his failure to put out meal worms for the birds. By his account his wife's death had been a bizarre accident. He had not seen her fall the first time, he claimed.

The second head injury could have come when he pushed her against the living-room window in the heat of the argument and the third one when he tried to stop her biting his finger after they had fallen onto the decking.

He said he had tidied bloody tissues and gloves away from the scene and changed his clothes and washed because they had agreed to pretend they'd been robbed when their daughter returned from school. He claimed he not been hiding a crime.

On Friday, January 29, 2010, Lillis was convicted of the manslaughter of Celine Cawley after the jury had deliberated for nine hours and 28 minutes. Ten days later Lillis was sentenced to six years and 11 months in jail – a sentence he has been serving at Dublin's Wheatfield Prison.

Imposing sentence at the Central Criminal Court, Mr Justice Barry White said it was clear from the victim-impact statements that the 52-year-old's behaviour had had a devastating effect on many people.

He said the jury had clearly rejected his contention that he bore no responsibility for his wife's death.

Mr Justice White said that at least Eamonn Lillis had the decency to call the emergency services – "the only decent act" Lillis had committed on the day of his wife's death, as far as the judge could see. Before that call was made, Lillis had taken time to hide clothes in the attic and make up a story about a burglary, he added.

Mr Justice White said that account was repeated in the days following the death and Lillis even went so far as to point the finger of suspicion at an innocent man. He said that even though gardai afforded him several chances to tell the truth, the lie had persisted until he was charged and taken into custody. Judge White said he considered it appropriate he should consider Lillis's lies and cover-up and their effect on the Cawley family.

While in prison, Lillis has focused much of his attention on artistic pursuits, including painting and his high-profile involvement in a play watched by President Michael D Higgins in the spring of 2012. He also wrote an essay which won an award in the Listowel Writers' Week in June 2012.

Lillis may well take solace in his artistic endeavours because his sinister crime means he is now isolated from many of those he was closest to before being locked up.

These include his daughter, Georgia, who stated in a 2011 court case over the family assets that she would rather "stick pins in her eyes" than see her father return to the family home where he murdered her beloved mother.

In May 2012 Lillis was stripped of his plush holiday villa by a French court. A French judge ruled he was "unworthy" of keeping the exclusive property which he co-owned with his late wife. Their daughter, Georgia, aged 19 at the time, became sole owner of the €800,000 property in Hossegor, southern France.

Earlier in 2012, Georgia and Celine's family lost a High Court case to stop Lillis from inheriting cash and properties in Ireland.

Assets that Celine and Lillis jointly owned included the French holiday home, their five-bedroom home in Howth – now valued at €1 million because of the property crash – a €180,000 apartment in nearby Sutton and €68,000 in investments. If both these properties are sold, the killer will receive more than €600,000 upon his release from jail.

It is unlikely to compensate him for the life he threw away when he battered in his wife's head with a brick.

CHAPTER 11

Cold Blooded Killers

It took 23 long years for justice to come for the killers of Bernard Brian McGrath — a tragic figure who was slaughtered in cold blood by his wife and son-in-law in the spring of 1987 in rural Co Westmeath.

The convictions of English national Colin Pinder and the victim's twisted wife Vera have been the greatest triumph so far of the garda cold case unit — officially known as the Garda Serious Crime Review Team — which was set up almost exactly 20 years after Brian McGrath was savagely butchered. But this was a case that would never have been solved without advances in DNA technology which led to a definite identification of bones belonging to the victim which were exhumed from Whitehall Cemetery in Coole, Co Westmeath, on the morning of May 19, 2008.

Advances in the scientific area of forensic anthropology also played a key role in the investigation.

The ironic thing about the garda probe is that gardai had already known for 15 years by who and why Brian McGrath had been killed but the DPP had decided in 1993 that there was not enough evidence to go with the case.

When the Cold Case Unit was set up under the leadership of Detective Superintendent Christy Mangan in 2007, the Brian McGrath case became one of its first targets after a retired detective suggested that the unit should examine it and garda sources point out that "all the building blocks for a successful prosecution were already in place."

Dublin native Brian McGrath was a man who had lived a troubled life before he seemed to disappear without trace in March, 1987. He was discovered as an infant in August 1944, abandoned and wrapped in a tablecloth on the side of the road between Nobber, Co Meath and Carrickmacross, Co Monaghan. The abandoned child was taken in by nuns in Dundalk who gave him his name. Mr McGrath would later spend time at the industrial school in Artane, Co Dublin where like many children in that institution during the grim era of the early 1950s, he suffered a nightmarish childhood. It would be later revealed that he was terrified by the Christian Brothers who ran the school and his daughter Veronica would later claim that her murdered dad had told her he was forced to eat from a pig trough because he was so hungry on at least one occasion.

He would meet his future wife Vera in 1960 when he was aged 16 and she was 12. Shortly afterwards he joined the British army and served abroad for a few years. After his return to Ireland, he got together with Vera. The couple moved to London where they were married in 1966 in a church near Holloway Road in the English capital. Like many Irish emigrants he worked on the building sites while she worked in a cigarette factory for a while before becoming pregnant.

They returned to Ireland two years later after the birth of their first child Veronica, staying with Vera's mother in Finglas. It wasn't long before they emigrated again, this time to Wales, where they worked on a farm. They had three other children; Andrew, Brian Jnr and Edward. Eventually they returned to Dublin, where they lived at a number of addresses before their nomadic life style came to an end when they moved to a bungalow on the outskirts of Coole, a sleepy rural village near Castlepollard, Co Westmeath and Granard, Co Longford, in 1979.

While there Brian McGrath did occasional 'casual work' for local farmers and at first it seemed that the family were living an idyllic, simple and happy life in the heart of the country. But cracks were soon to appear in this seemingly happy existence. The marriage between Brian and Vera McGrath became more and more stormy — violence began to feature. Gardai and a local doctor were called to the home on a number of occasions. Vera McGrath took her children to women's refuges several times during the early to mid-1980s but always returned to her husband in Co Westmeath.

Local GP Dr Patrick Cullen would later recall that he had made emergency call-outs to the McGrath house three or four times during this extremely turbulent period in the mid-80s. Two years before the murder Dr Cullen was called to the house in Lower Coole on March 6, 1985. He said that when he arrived at the house Mr McGrath was in a very agitated state and the atmosphere was volatile. He removed Mr McGrath to diffuse the situation and he decided to commit Brian McGrath to the St Loman's Mental Hospital in Mullingar, Co Westmeath.

According to documentation from his committal in St Loman's, Mr McGrath was "aggressive, agitated and paranoid". Dr Cullen noted in a cover letter that both the wife and daughter seemed "petrified" and the daughter had "bruises ++" -- medical shorthand for abundant and visible marks. The doctor was told by Vera and Veronica McGrath that Brian McGrath had delusions and hallucinations, and had changed into a violent person, becoming violent over mundane events. They complained of recurrent recent assaults by him. The doctor had filled in the committal form in the presence of Vera McGrath, who signed a section stating that her husband was not capable of deciding whether to enter hospital voluntarily. Dr Cullen had signed another section stating that he was of the opinion that Mr McGrath required mental treatment and was unfit as a voluntary patient. Three weeks earlier on February 20th, 1985, the doctor had also been called to the house and he had later filled out a form as part of garda requirements where he noted "Wife has multiple bruising following alleged assaults". He had described Mr McGrath as "aggressive, agitated and annoyed".

Brian McGrath was ultimately committed to the St Loman's institution after Dr Cullen wrote that he "is not in my opinion capable of entering hospital voluntarily". The form was signed by Mrs McGrath, who had applied for his committal. A neighbour, Michael White would later tell gardai that Mr McGrath was a changed man when he came out of the mental hospital – appearing to be much more withdrawn. Mr White had of course been aware that gardai were called to the McGrath home on several occasions during those times. He saw at first hand that Brian and Vera McGrath had a volatile relationship. On one occasion, they rowed on their way to visit him and had "kicked the shins off each other".

Another neighbour Mary Manning would later tell gardai that she saw Vera dressing Brian in women's clothes and calling a doctor to say he was going mad. She said the local doctor was then called and came to find Mr McGrath in bed wearing a skirt and black tights. What can't be doubted is what was happening in the Co Westmeath homestead was truly dysfunctional in nature.

The family's oldest daughter Veronica left the family home for the UK in the midst of this madness when she turned 18 with an older man. This relationship broke up but she then began seeing Colin Pinder, a man from Liverpool whom she met in England but decided to move back to Co Westmeath with him in February 1987.

The couple moved to Co Westmeath and lived in a caravan on a neighbouring land but the situation would not get any better. Just days later, Dr Cullen was again called to the McGrath home, where a "shouting match" was in progress involving Mr and Mrs McGrath and their daughter Veronica. Two gardai also arrived from Granard station in Co Longford to deal with the situation.

There was no sign of physical violence on that occasion, but Dr Cullen decided to get Brian McGrath a bed for the night in a nearby holiday home.

It is not known when exactly Brian McGrath was murdered but it was definitely on a night between March 16, 1987 and April 18, of that same year.

Incredibly it would be another six years before gardai realised he had been killed. It would be 1993 before the terrible secret got exposed but even then justice would take another 17 years to come.

Wracked by guilt and coerced by a new partner who she had told her terrible secret to, Veronica went first to a social worker, then to English police and finally to gardai and told them that her dad had been killed by her mother and her then-fiancé Colin Pinder.

She told stunned officers the details of what was truly a gore fest — it had previously been thought that Brian McGrath had fled to Holland from all the aggravation in his family life — a lie which had been spread by her mother Vera. What Veronica had to say about the night that her dad was murdered was truly disturbing. Veronica gave a detailed description of her father's death, alleging Mr Pinder had killed her father in a prolonged attack, urged on by her mother.

At the murder trial 17 years later, she went through this statement in the witness box as a hushed court room listened to the gruesome horror. Ms McGrath said her mother visited her and Pinder in their caravan on a neighbour's land one evening while her father went into the neighbour's house.

"(My mother) said that she wished my father was dead and that they had been fighting," testified a soft-spoken Ms McGrath.

"My mother said to Colin that he wouldn't be man enough to kill my father," she continued after a number of pauses. "He said that he had the very thing and produced a spanner. He said that one blow of this would be enough."

She said that her mother was gesturing to Mr Pinder as all four of them walked back to the McGrath home, where her three younger brothers were sleeping. The house was locked and her mother got in a window to let them in the back door.

"Colin moved his arm and I seen the top of the spanner. He then hit my father. He hit him at the back of the head," she said. "My father fell to the ground."

She recalled that her mother came out of the house with tools in her hand. "One was a slash hook and the other was like a long monkey wrench. She handed them to Colin Pinder."

She said that Pinder hit her father several times with the slash hook while her father pleaded with him. "He was saying: 'Have mercy on me.' Several times he asked for mercy," she said.

She said she was then told to go inside and turn up the radio. When she returned, she said, her father was trying to defend himself with a wooden ladder by throwing it at Pinder. She said her father ran onto a bóithrín where her fiancé hit him on the legs with the slash hook. She recalled seeing her father standing in the ditch and Mr Pinder hitting the ditch with the implement.

"I went into the ditch and my father said to me his eyes were stinging and he couldn't see. I thought his face didn't look right. I thought one side of his face looked very distorted." She said her mother was standing in this laneway as her father begged for his car keys.

"Let me go. I would do anything," he pleaded, according to his daughter. "Just give me the keys of my car. I'll go and leave ye the house and everything." She said that the next time she saw her father he was on the ground at the top of the lane.

"He appeared very, very still, like he was all curled up," she said."The next thing I recollect he was at the back of the garage," she said, recalling him make a gurgling sound. "I asked my mother what it was and she said it was called the death rattle." Veronica said she also remembered her mother hit her father that night, with a lump hammer.

"I know that Colin and my mother were laughing at the way she hit him," she said.

Ms McGrath said that her fiancé and mother then carried her father up the garden in a blanket and she did not see him alive again. "They put him in a shallow grave at the top of the field," she said, recalling that they covered him with galvanised sheeting. She said she stayed in the kitchen that night and must have drifted off to sleep. "I remember my mother shaking me by the arm, saying that there was a big mess or things were bad outside," she said. Her mother asked her to clean blood and white mucus off the walls but she could not so her mother told her to put tar on it.

As part of the pretence after the murder, just two days after the slaying, Veronica and her mother visited a solicitor in Granard, Co Longford, to obtain a barring order against the dead man. As part of the act Veronica gave her mother a love bite on the check to make it look like she had been bruised from a severe beating. Ms McGrath married Colin Pinder on April 18 1987, after which they lived in her parents' home. Soon afterwards her mother took Veronica's three younger male siblings to England for a couple of months before returning to Lower Coole.

"My father was dug up from where he was," she recalled. "There was a fire. It was a big fire, which went on for a couple of days. For the first day, there was a very bad smell." She said she went over to the fire at least once. She later explained that she saw a 'very bright, glowing orange circular object' on a two-pronged pitch fork being held by Pinder beside the fire.

"I took it that it was my father's head," she said. "I seen my father's rib cage," she explained. "Both Colin and my mother were sifting through the fire and bringing particles of my father down to the house in a biscuit tin," she testified. "Some went into the range and some went into the septic tank."

Veronica had a baby boy in 1987, split with Pinder in 1988 and moved to England. She told her story to a social worker in 1993 after coming under pressure from her then-partner, and the British police were contacted. She travelled to Ireland that year and gave her statements to the Gardai which in turn led to the arrest of her mother Vera and later Colin Pinder. The Garda investigation was led at this stage by Det Sgt Aidan Glacken — one of the midlands' most experienced detectives at the time and now a chief superintendent in charge of the Meath garda division.

After getting a statement from Veronica, gardai met Vera by appointment on November 12, 1993, and she gave them a 14-page voluntary statement outlining her version of events on the night of the murder. In her statement to officers, Vera recalled that on one night in March, 1987, she went down to the caravan in which her daughter and Colin Pinder lived in with letters for Veronica.

She told her daughter and Pinder that her husband was still fighting with her and said, "I wish he was dead." She then claimed Pinder said, "I've just the thing to do it," and he produced a kind of a silver thing with a knob on it, but told them that they would all have to agree about it.

"I must've been out of my mind, but I agreed," Vera told gardai, adding they had all shaken hands on it. According to her account, later that evening, when they got to the house, they found themselves locked out. Vera got in her bedroom window and was standing in the room when she heard a bang, 'like a thud'. Looking out the window, she saw her husband's body on the ground. Pinder kept telling her that she would have to hit him as well. Eventually, she did hit him and there was no further sound. She went back into the house. Then Pinder ran in to say her husband 'wasn't there anymore'.

Her statement continued that Pinder found him in the turf shed. She saw her husband run down the driveway but claimed Pinder caught him, hitting him at least twice with a slash-hook on the legs, she said. Pinder followed him into the hedge and she saw him raise the slash-hook again. Then he said, "it's all over" and the three of them carried the body wrapped in Mr Pinder's coat up to the house, she said. Vera said she heard a 'rattling or gurgling sound' which she took to be his dying gasp.

Pinder then hit Mr McGrath in a frenzy with a small concrete mould 20 or 30 times, she told gardai. He told the girl that he had done it "for you, because I love you". They buried the body in a shallow grave and, the next morning, Vera and Veronica cleaned up the mess outside. There was blood, thick clots and mucus on the wall of the shed, she said.

A few days after, Vera went to the UK with her sons, returning about seven weeks later. "We decided to destroy the body by burning (it)," she told gardai and, the day after her return, Pinder lit "a big blaze". Afterwards, Pinder told them there was still some of the body left and began to break it up with a pitchfork, while Vera and Veronica banged with shovels, until she told him she couldn't do it anymore.

The next step in the jigsaw for gardai was tracking down Colin Pinder and they got English police to take a statement from him in a Yorkshire police station. Pinder — a man of mixed race who had also had an extremely tough life — also co-operated with the investigation and gave a voluntary statement six years after he was involved in the killing. He said he had moved to Coole, Co Westmeath, with Veronica McGrath and was planning to marry her. Initially they had been invited to live with her parents but her father then provided them with a caravan on a friend's land instead.

He said that Mrs McGrath invited them to stay in the house when her husband was away for a couple of days and that Brian McGrath 'blew up' when he returned to find the couple there with her.

"You get out with your ni**er boyfriend," said Mr McGrath, according to Pinder's account of events. He claimed that Mr McGrath then began to push him out. "I just lost my temper and I hit him quite hard," he continued. "He spun around and fell down and hit the corner of the range with his head. There was like a dent in his forehead."

He said Mr McGrath was bleeding but not breathing and he thought he had killed him. Both women were screaming, he added. Pinder said he suggested getting the police and telling the truth but that Mrs McGrath said not to involve them. She said 'No-one will ask any questions because he's always going off. People are being murdered in the North all the time'. "They sort of had me convinced," he said. "I stupidly agreed to bury him in the field."

He said he dug a shallow hole, they put him in and covered him with soil. He claimed that over the following week Mrs McGrath suggested moving the body and digging a deeper hole, but he refused.

"I couldn't face going through it all again," he explained. "That week was hell. We were just arguing." He said he married Ms McGrath a few weeks later; the date had already been set. It was some time after that that he agreed to move and burn the body.

"We done it in the night time," he said, explaining that he felt "terrible" when he dug up the body. He said he lit the fire and they went into the house for a few hours while it burned. He said they returned, moved the ashes with a spade and put soil on top. He said he left Ireland about a month later, two weeks after his new bride gave birth to their child. This was at the request of both mother and daughter, he said.

"I'm really sick about it all. I'm sick that I did it and I'm sorry," he concluded in his statement.

After getting all these statements gardai then conducted a major search of the property at Coole in November, 1993, and found bones at the site. Vera McGrath was arrested while officers searched the three-quarter acre garden. Again she co-operated with officers while being held at Mullingar Garda Station.

Detective Garda James Campbell was involved in the grim search of the family's back garden in 1993. He would later tell Vera McGrath and Colin Pinder's murder trial that his team dug for half an hour before coming across the charred remains of a fire, covered by six inches of clay. He told the court: "We removed the clay and started to search minutely with trowels. I found pieces of bone and cloth and some teeth, which appeared to be human. Also, Garda Roger Nicholson uncovered a jaw bone with the teeth still intact."

Garda Kieran Williams said at the trial that after they got down on their hands and knees he found particles of apparently blood-stained cloth.

"I came across small particles of bone that looked like bones from a finger" he would later recall.

Retired ballistics expert Sergeant Edwin Hancock was also present when a steel crowbar was recovered from the septic tank, along with bones and a gent's watch. Sgt Hancock also found Irish coins from 1970, 1978 and 1982 during his search of the burnt area. A kitchen knife and Stanley knife were found in a cavity of the garage wall, which seemed to be daubed with a tar-like substance, he said. He could not remove this material so had the affected blocks removed instead.

Anatomist Dr Patrick Felle was drafted in by gardai for the search and he found bone fragments in the garden when he sifted through a lot of material that also included chicken and sheep bones before identifying the human bones.

"The vast amount was fragmented and had been chopped up," he said, explaining that only the small bones of the right hand and some small foot bones were intact.

He said that much of the bone was also burnt but this hand and part of the jaw bone was not.

"It looked likely that they were from one human. We didn't find two of anything," he would later recall adding that he was also able to tell that the deceased had been more than 25 years old. He said that the thickness of the bones was consistent with them having belonged to a male of average build, but he could not be certain as so much of the pelvis was missing.

Although he had been provided with Brian McGrath's dental chart, the teeth and jaw particles found were not from the part of the mouth that had been charted. Dr Felle said about a third of the vertebrae had been found, along with 5-10% of the total rib mass. No sternum was found and only a small percentage of the pelvis. There was no collar bone or shoulder blade and none of the left arm was recovered.

Amazingly despite all this evidence and the three incriminating statements about the murder which had been obtained by gardai, the DPP decided there was not enough evidence to prosecute the case.

DNA profiling was at its infancy in 1993 and the bones could not be positively identified. Brian McGrath's bones were placed in a bucket within a coffin and buried in an unmarked grave in Whitehall Cemetery in Coole in 1994.

Two years later in November, 1996, Vera McGrath's solicitor even received a letter from the-then Superintendent in Granard informing her that she would not be prosecuted in relation to Brian McGrath's supposed death. "I confirm that the garda investigation into this case has concluded," the letter read.

It seemed to be a strange end to a very disturbing saga but everything changed in January, 2008, when the garda cold case decided to re-investigate it.

Det Sgt Michael Buckley reviewed the file of the murder investigation He received DNA samples from Mr McGrath's sons and bones found when their father's remains were exhumed in May, 2008, were positively identified as Mr McGrath's.

Consultant anthropologist Laureen Buckley — whose groundbreaking work has been used in dozens of murder investigations — found one human bone at the McGrath home in Lower Coole in May, 2008, after the Cold Case Review Team decided it should be searched again.

She later told the murder trial that the bones found in 1993 were exhumed from a cemetery and she examined all the remains with State Pathologist Dr Marie Cassidy.

"About 50 per cent of the skeleton was recovered," she said, assuming Mr McGrath was a slightly built man. She said that she was able to tell that the bones came from a male by the pronounced brow ridge. She explained that bone is brownish in colour but turns black when heated by fire. It turns grey and finally white when completely burnt. The bones she examined varied from unburnt to completely cremated, Ms Buckley said at the murder trial.

Meanwhile, by this stage Det Sgt Michael Buckley had travelled to Liverpool where he interviewed Colin Pinder who again admitted his role in the killing, pointing out that Brian McGrath was violent towards his family and racially abusive to him.

"I'm not a murderer. I just wanted to give him a good hiding," he explained. "I'm in bits since this. I'm prepared to do time for what I did but not for murder," he said at the end of the interview. "I feel a lot of remorse for what I've done." Pinder told the gardai he would face any charges here without them needing a European Arrest Warrant.

Det Sgt Buckley later recalled that Pinder came to Dublin in February, 2009 to clarify some issues.

"I tried to kill myself twice because of this two years ago," Pinder told the highly-respected detective. On February 6, 2009, Pinder was charged with Brian McGrath's murder — he had long since split up from Veronica McGrath, who was to go on to have successive children with multiple partners.

Veronica was granted immunity from prosecution for her role in the crime on condition that she give evidence against her mother and former husband. Her mother Vera was charged with the murder on May, 12, 2009, after a dramatic appearance at Longford District Court.

The duo went on trial at Dublin's Central Criminal Court in June, 2010, and after a marathon five-week case which was full of truly shocking evidence, Pinder was convicted of manslaughter while Vera McGrath was found guilty of murder at the age of 61 and is now serving a life sentence in the Dochas Women's Prison in Dublin. Colin Pinder was aged 47 when he was jailed for nine years for Mr McGrath's manslaughter in December, 2010.

Mr Justice John Edwards described the killing of Bernard Brian McGrath (43) by Pinder and the victim's wife as "callous and vicious." Mr Justice Edwards described as "savage, depraved and barbaric" the manner in which Mr McGrath's body was desecrated after the killing.

Great effort was made to conceal the body, noted the judge, with the ashes scattered and any remaining bones splintered and put into drains and a septic tank. The judge said this had caused much distress to the victim's family, excluding Vera and Veronica McGrath, whom the court treated as an accessory after the fact. Mr Justice Edwards said the distress was felt by Mr McGrath's three sons, who were children at the time.

The sons — Brian, Andrew and Edward McGrath — were led to believe that they had been abandoned by their father, whom they remembered as being kind, hard-working and intelligent. The judge described the victim impact statement they gave to his court as poignant. They said that the way their father's life had been taken was barbaric and had left them numb with shock. They had been unable to grieve and mourn in a natural way and had been deprived of a father figure in their life.

This was the first murder conviction for the garda's Cold case unit. Det Supt Christy Mangan, who led the investigation, said it was significant for bereaved families and would give them hope. He said it was a complex investigation due to the passage of time, with some people unavailable to give evidence.

"It can be very difficult to get all the pieces of the jigsaw together in order to present it in a court for a prosecution," he said. "It is difficult but it has been done in this case and we're satisfied with what has taken place," he added.

He said it was a joint investigation between the detectives in Granard, led by Det Insp Martin Cadden, and the serious crime review team.

"It's as a result of the work done by both units that has brought this case to justice today, "he added.

He said the three McGrath brothers and their sister wanted justice for their father and that justice had been done. He said that although Brian McGrath died in 1987, he had been remembered now through the verdict. He also thanked the people of Coole for their help during the 17-year investigation. The work of the Cold Case unit continues with some high-profile cases due before the courts in the coming months.

CHAPTER 12

Blood On The Streets

The north inner city of Dublin has been plagued by two serious gangland feuds over the past six years — and one of these brutal gang wars has received far more publicity than the other.

This is the bitter fall-out between former criminal comrades centred around paedophile gangster Christy Griffin — who is serving a 15-year sentence for the rape of a former partner's teenage daughter. This feud has claimed five lives.

But an equally bitter gang war co-existed with the more high profile Christy Griffin feud and it has led to two savage gun murders as well as dozens of violent incidents.

Again, former friends and associates turned on each other but in this case it was when a petty row over a woman spiralled out of control.

The main protagonists were Paul 'Paulie' Kelly and Michael Taylor Jnr and one of the most savage nights in the warfare happened on April 6, 2007 at Winston Ville apartments on Charlemont Road in Clontarf, north Dublin, when Kelly was riddled with gun shots by Taylor and one of his associates in a brutal attack.

It was 11.50pm on Good Friday, 2007, when Paul Kelly came out of the apartment block where he had lived for just a few weeks.

Kelly — who had earlier sent a text to an unidentified man — was shot a total of 11 times and suffered horrendous injuries in the brutal ambush.

Kelly — a small time 26-year-old criminal from Gardiner Street in the north inner city — knew that his life was in danger because of his feud with Taylor, a more serious criminal who he had been childhood friends with.

The murder victim had specialised in stealing high-powered cars and motorbikes. At the time of his savage death, he had a small number of convictions for theft and other minor offences. Kelly was also the prime suspect in a gun attack that left a teenager from Rutland Street with serious injuries in 2004. He was arrested as part of the Garda investigation but could not be charged because the victim withdrew his complaint.

The row stared in early 2006 when the two men had a major disagreement over a woman. In one of the first signs that this dispute was going to get very serious, Michael Taylor Jnr — then aged 26 — was caught by officers in the Croke Villas area of the northside with a knuckle-duster in his back pocket in October 2006.

He later admitted that he had the weapon for protection because of the feud.

Family members on both sides then got involved. Cars and motorbikes belonging to one side were damaged in a vandalism incident which directly led to Michael Taylor Jnr being stabbed three times while he walked in the north inner city with a small child. He received only minor injuries — but less than a week later the suspected knifeman Paul Kelly was shot dead in revenge.

And it truly was a savage killing as bullets were fired into Kelly from a handgun and shotgun.

A post-mortem examination showed multiple shotgun pellets in his head along with bullets in his trunk. The examination, conducted by Deputy State Pathologist Dr Michael Curtis, revealed a shotgun wound on Kelly's face extending from above his right eyebrow to his chin.

The second shotgun wound covered the back of his neck and shoulder. Both contained multiple pellet strikes, while similar pellet strikes to Kelly's right hand could have been associated with either of the shotgun wounds.

There were also a number of pellet strikes in his abdomen, ribcage and groin and lead pellets were found embedded in his left thigh and shin. Dr Curtis found 11 bullet wounds in total, including one in the right of Kelly's abdomen, two in his back and one in his right arm. One bullet had entered the right side of his face and exited his left temple and a single bullet had caused three wounds, entering the back of his right thigh, exiting the groin and re-entering nearby.

A wound to his upper abdomen was bigger than the others and Dr Curtis believed it to be a double entry wound, caused by two bullets. In all, he would later tell Taylor's murder trial that he recovered eight bullets from the body, along with a number of shotgun pellets. The pathologist said that bones in the victim's skull were shattered and that the under-surface of his brain and his brain stem were lacerated. His lower jaw was also shattered and several of his teeth were detached and broken.

He said Kelly's left jugular was lacerated from gunshot wounds, his lung was wounded and the sack around the heart was lacerated.

"The heart muscle was extensively lacerated," Dr Curtis continued. "One of the main coronary arteries had been cut across by a bullet." He added that part of the liver was also extensively lacerated. Dr Curtis said that the catastrophic injuries to Kelly's brain, jugular, lung and liver were incompatible with life and gave his cause of death as multiple gunshot wounds.

This was truly a targeted gangland assassination and hours before Dr Curtis had carried out his grim medical examination on Kelly's body, gardai had already made extremely significant progress.

It was a murder that sent shockwaves through the capital on what was a gloriously sunny Easter weekend. It led to the Catholic Archbishop of Dublin issuing a stinging indictment of the capital's culture of gangland violence and the "never-ending cascade of retribution" during the Easter Vigil Mass in the Pro-Cathedral.

Addressing his congregation, Dr Diarmuid Martin said: "We see again the terrible domino process of how responding to evil by evil only generates in its turn another act of evil, a never-ending cascade of retribution.

"I remind once again all those who believe that they can impose their rule by violence that all they are doing is closing themselves into the grip of a violence from which there is no way out. The way of violence leads only to death."

How right the Archbishop's words were — but by the time that he had spoken them, gardai had made great progress, significantly arresting Michael Taylor and his dad Michael Taylor Snr as well as three of their close associates, including a woman.

Officers had been alerted to the gun attack by 999 calls made by shocked people who lived in or near the Winston Ville apartment complex in Clontarf. These people would all later give statements to detectives. One such resident lived on the top floor of a building on the corner of Charlemont Road and Cecil Avenue at the time. He was in bed about 11.45pm that night when he heard two loud bangs, which he first thought were just fireworks. However, when he heard more rapid bangs after a pause, he thought it was more sinister and looked out his window.

"I saw two gentlemen in balaclavas running down the road," he told detectives, explaining that they turned off Charlemont Road onto Cecil Avenue. "One looked like he had a shotgun or iron bar. The other had a handgun. One was taller, the other shorter and stockier."

He said he then heard a car being revved and it seemed to take off at speed along the Malahide Road. He dialled 999 before also hearing a woman screaming. Another neighbour described hearing sounds such as "two bangs and then repeat noises", like a car backfiring. He said he then heard a crash, which he thought was a windscreen being smashed, and went to his front door.

"Two guys ran out of the lane, I thought they were at the cars," he said of the men, who were wearing balaclavas and black gloves. He shouted at them and one of them told him to "shut the f**k up", he said.

"They turned towards me and I saw the guns, a sawn-off shotgun and a pistol," he said. "So I moved back into the house and shut the door." He said he then heard screaming and, having done first aid, he ran out to see if someone was hurt. He found a man slumped on the floor inside the entrance to the Winston Ville apartments.

"I saw brain blood, that dark blood," he said. "I knew there was nothing I could do."

And there was indeed no hope for Paul Kelly after he became the victim of such a ferocious double gun attack. Within minutes the area was flooded by gardai, and Garda Pauraic McInerney was one of the first officers there — and he immediately began searching the area for evidence.

He found a black glove at the junction of Charlemont Road and Cecil Avenue, where the two men in balaclavas had been seen running — this would later prove to be a highly significant discovery.

Detective Aidan Dardis from the Garda ballistics section recovered a number of shotgun pellets and wadding from the scene. He also found 12 discharged cartridge cases from a 9mm weapon.

Detective Sergeant David Gallagher was one of dozens of officers at the murder scene at 12.20am on April 7 when he got a call to Innisfallen Road in nearby Drumcondra, where a colleague had stopped a black Saab which had been acting suspiciously.

"I arrested Michael Taylor Snr on suspicion of unlawful possession of firearms at Winston Ville apartments," he later recalled at the murder trial — referring to Michael Taylor's father.

At around the same time Michael Taylor Jnr was picked up in the north inner city — detectives at this stage had been briefed about the ongoing feud. Later that morning, Det Sgt Gallagher was part of a team that searched a house in Rutland Court in the city. There he arrested a male friend of the Taylors also on suspicion of unlawful possession of firearms at Winston Ville apartments.

There were four people in the house on Rutland Court when it was searched and gardai seized a number of mobile phones from the property including one linked to Michael Taylor Jnr. It would be analysis of this phone that would play a huge role in Michael Taylor Jnr's subsequent conviction for murder.

Investigations later established that three different numbers were linked to the same headset — Michael Taylor Jnr had previously rang a garda in Crumlin Station on one of those numbers.

It was also established that a phone used by Taylor was using a mobile phone mast near the crime scene around the time of the murder. In fact, this number used a phone mast in Clontarf four times around the time of the murder. It would be a number of months after the murder that DNA would also link Michael Taylor Jnr to the crime after a black glove found at the scene was forensically analysed.

Forensic scientist Dr Dorothy Ramsbottom obtained a mixture of DNA from the inside of the glove, with a major male component and a minor component. This meant there was DNA from two people on the glove.

She was able to generate a full DNA profile from the major component and this matched Taylor's profile. She would later tell his murder trial that the chances of an unrelated person having the same profile was less than one in 1,000 million, but that a close blood relative would be more likely to share the profile.

Dr Ramsbottom also conceded that she could not say when the DNA was deposited in the glove or which person had worn the glove more recently.

Meanwhile, after three days of questioning and forensic testing at various northside stations, all five suspects who had been arrested for the murder had been released without charge. But the feud remained very active.

Six weeks after the murder, associates of Paul Kelly were involved in a revenge attack in which a military grenade was thrown onto the rear balcony of a flat at Rutland Court in the Summerhill area of Dublin on the night of May 23, 2007. There were ten people, including children, in the Taylor home at the time — watching a football match when the device exploded and blew out windows as well as damaging rear patio doors and the kitchen. But nobody was hurt.

Gardai called in an Army bomb disposal team who examined the remnants of the grenade. The previous night, associates of the Taylor and Kelly families had clashed in Dublin's Mater Hospital when one family was visiting a relative of Kelly. One woman was stabbed in the hand and received superficial injuries while a man sustained head wounds after being struck during the scuffle.

Michael Taylor Snr appeared at Dublin District Court in May 2009 on minor public order charges in relation to the hospital brawl when he agreed to keep the peace for two years as a condition of the charges being struck out.

What was happening between these two factions in the north inner city — combined with the separate Christy Griffin feud — made north inner city Dublin one of the most heavily policed areas in western Europe at the time.

The area was subject to almost constant policing by the heavily armed Garda Emergency Response Unit with the Garda helicopter providing regular assistance from the air.

Garda management felt saturation policing was the only way to prevent further bloodshed or even a massacre — as the grenade attack could easily have been. And all during this period, officers in Clontarf Garda Station backed up by specialist units such as the National Bureau of Criminal Investigation (NBCI) and detectives from other Dublin stations continued with their intensive investigation into Paul Kelly's murder.

On July 26, 2007, Sgt Joe O'Flaherty stopped a Ford Focus reversing at speed out of Rutland Court into Buckingham Street — close to Michael Taylor Snr's house.

There had been a grenade thrown into the rear of the house on the previous day. He spoke with Michael Taylor Jnr, who was with the driver Stephen Keogh. Taylor told him that the feud was over. The families had met and negotiated a peace deal.

Sgt O'Flaherty put this detail into the Garda Pulse system. He felt this was good news as the community had been at risk. This evidence would be later used as part of Michael Taylor Jnr's murder trial as proof that a feud was in fact taking place — something which Taylor tried to deny any knowledge of when he went on trial.

As the months went by the situation showed no sign of calming down. In December 2007, a close female associate of Paul Kelly was caught with a loaded pistol as she drove through the north inner city. The woman, in her 30s, was later given a three-year suspended sentence after Dublin Circuit Criminal Court heard she got the gun after her associate was shot dead and there were serious threats against her life.

She would later have to flee the violence in Dublin and re-locate to Co Cavan with her family. By this stage, Michael Taylor Jnr's life of gangland crime had caught up with him as gardai continued to mount regular operations against him and his gang.

On August 23, 2007 — four months after the murder of Paul Kelly — armed gardai set up a special surveillance operation at Sandyford Business Park after getting information about plans for an armed cash-in-transit robbery. Michael Taylor and his older associate Graham Byrne were caught in possession of a 9mm pistol, which had a bullet in the breech ready to be fired, when gardai found them sitting in a stolen van parked directly opposite the steel door of the strong room at AIB in Sandyford Business Park that morning.

Another associate, Stephen Fagan, was found with a radio scanner tuned into Garda and Securicor radio frequencies sitting in another stolen vehicle nearby and tried to ram the Garda patrol cars that had blocked him in. All three were wearing two sets of clothing and gloves. The cash-in-transit van was loaded with €200,000 cash and the staff were due to remove a further €54,000 from the ATM when gardai — who had mounted a surveillance operation as a result of confidential information — intervened so as to save any possible injury or threat to lives.

Gardai found Taylor wearing a balaclava in the van at Sandyford Business Park and noticed a second balaclava on the van floor, while Fagan had two sets of car keys belonging to stolen vehicles, which were later found parked nearby with false registration plates fitted.

Both Taylor and Byrne relied on their right to silence during the Garda interviews while Fagan said he was there to "pick up something for someone" to whom he said he "owed €100,000" because he lost drugs he had been holding.

Fagan admitted being in possession of the stolen car but denied knowing both Byrne and Taylor and claimed he had not been involved in the planned robbery. Taylor appeared before Dublin Circuit Court on November 10, 2008, in relation to these charges, where he and the two other criminals pleaded guilty.

In that court appearance Taylor also pleaded guilty to possession of cocaine worth €70,000 for sale or supply after gardai caught him in what was described as "a drug-mixing factory" at a Garrettstown, north Co Dublin, house on July 26, 2006.

On that occasion, gardai found a kilo of cocaine, 29 bags of mixing agent, a blender and mixing bowls laid out on a table in the Garrettstown house. In a sign of just how intertwined Dublin gangs are, the 2006 drugs bust was a special Garda operation aimed at the gang which was led by slain drugs trafficker Michael 'Micka' Kelly — the gangster murdered by the Real IRA in September 2010.

In court two years after the Garrettstown drugs bust, Taylor's lawyer said he "owed €1,300" to this gang — even though the mob were not mentioned in court — as a result of a so-called "drug debt" and he had agreed to buy a blender and mixing bowls for the operation.

A detective in court also agreed with Taylor's lawyer's suggestion that it "could be possible" that senior members of this gang asked Taylor to give them the book of evidence in this case to check if his admissions had identified them. In total, Taylor was jailed by Judge Katherine Delahunt for 13 years in consecutive sentences for his role in these two very serious gangland related crimes. There can be little doubt that such a hefty jail sentence dismayed the criminal but worse was to come for him just 11 months later.

In late September 2009, gardai entered Mountjoy Prison and re-arrested Michael Taylor. He was brought to the Bridewell Courts complex where, on September 23, 2009, he was charged with Paul Kelly's murder two-and-a-half years earlier. With Taylor and many of his closest associates locked up and with many of the crew linked to Paul Kelly being forced to flee their north inner city homes, it seemed that the bitter feud had finally calmed down.

But those involved in serious gangland activity have very long memories and Michael Taylor's dad would pay the ultimate price in June 2011 for his son's crimes as well as his perceived involvement in the Paul Kelly murder — well over four years after Kelly was 'whacked' and just four months before his son was due to go on trial for murder.

Not long before Michael Taylor Snr was shot dead in front of his partner in broad daylight at a caravan park in Donabate, north Co Dublin, gardai received confidential information about his role in the Clontarf slaying of Kelly. At the murder trial in the absence of the jury, it was revealed that Det Sgt John McLoughlin had been informed by a member of the Kelly family that Michael Taylor Snr had arranged by telephone for a named man to drive the killers away from the scene of Paul Kelly's murder.

But, when interviewed, this man denied any involvement and expressed fears for his life which gardai believed were realistic. Mobile phone records were not available because of the time delay. The informant refused, on or off the record, to reveal the source of the information. What this shows is that associates of Paul Kelly believed that Michael Taylor Snr was involved in the murder.

On the evening of June 6, 2011, Taylor Snr was relaxing at his holiday home in Hand's Caravan Park, 300 metres from Donabate beach, on what had all the trappings of a peaceful Bank Holiday Monday.

Two men wearing balaclavas and dressed in grey and black hooded tops entered the caravan park and attacked Taylor, firing at least four shots, shortly after the victim arrived at the caravan park with his partner, who witnessed the horror, at 4.40pm. He was hit in the head and chest and was rushed to the intensive care unit at Beaumont Hospital where his condition was described as critical. His partner screamed when she heard the shots and ran crying towards the attackers, according to witnesses.

A witness at the scene said he heard four or five bangs and screaming. He saw the partner of the injured man run after the two shooters and then run back to her husband who lay on the ground outside the caravan.

"He had just got out of his car and I heard four or five shots," the witness said. "Next I heard screaming, 'He's been shot, he's been shot.' I rang 999 and told them what happened. He had blood on his head and a hole in his back. He had his eyes open. He was twisting and turning. He just seemed to be moaning."

The men ran away in the direction of Donabate beach and

got into a stolen metallic blue Opel Insignia, with an 09-D registration, in which they travelled to nearby Turvey Woods. The vehicle was then set on fire and the men left in a black Honda Civic hatchback with an 07-D registration which was later found in Glasnevin in Dublin's northside.

"This was a callous shooting, carried out in a reckless fashion," said Superintendent Mark Curran, who was in charge of the investigation. "It was reckless in the sense that there were bullets that were discharged that didn't hit the target, other than the victim. One was a car, the other went through the window of another caravan. There were in excess of four shots fired," he explained.

Supt Curran said gardai believed there were people in the caravan that was hit and said "lives were possibly put at risk".

Taylor died the following morning in Dublin's Beaumont Hospital and while no-one has ever been charged with the murder, gardai are certain that it was directly linked to the 2007 murder of Paul Kelly. The 2011 shooting meant tensions in the north inner city were at a heightened state yet again and armed Garda patrols were on the streets again, particularly in the days around the dead man's funeral.

Michael Taylor Jnr went on trial for Paul Kelly's murder in late October 2011, and he was convicted of the crime after the jury were told by the prosecution that they could use evidence of motive, DNA and mobile phone use together to convict the defendant of murder.

Colm O'Briain BL said the first strand was motive. He pointed out that there were bad relations between Michael Taylor and his family and Paul Kelly and his family, reminding the jury of evidence a garda had given in relation to the feud. He said the second strand of evidence related to mobile phones. He used a large number of phone records to argue that a phone number used on the night belonged to the accused.

He reminded the jury that this number used a phone mast in Clontarf four times around the time of the murder. "It's the prosecution's case that Michael Taylor was in the area with his phone, with his motive at the time Mr Kelly was so unceremoniously killed," he said.

The third strand of evidence, he said, was the glove found along the route taken by the killers as they fled the scene. "As you know, that glove was analysed," he said, reminding the jury that DNA matching the defendant's was found on the inside of the glove.

He finished his closing speech by saying that separately these pieces of evidence might not be enough to convict a person. "However, it is the prosecution's contention that when you combine the three strands of evidence, that you can be satisfied beyond a reasonable doubt that the accused, Michael Taylor, murdered Mr Kelly," he concluded.

After a nine-day trial, the jury deliberated for five-and-a-half hours before finding that Michael Taylor Jnr was guilty of murder by a majority verdict of ten to two members.

Taylor shook his head when the jury announced their decision. Who knows whether he thought of his dad — who had also been murdered as part of the bitter feud — at that moment.

In a victim impact statement which was read to the court when Taylor was handed the mandatory life sentence for murder, Paul Kelly's mother Bernie wrote: "On the 6th of April 2007, just before midnight, I received a call that was to shatter my life forever." She said her only son, the youngest of the family, but also the man of the family, had been taken from her. She said she could no longer bear to be around her daughters or grandchildren as it felt wrong without her son.

She said although she was on medication for her cancer, "I pray God will take me to my baby." She said that the family received her son home in a coffin on his daughter's seventh birthday, and she went to the church on her Communion day so he would see her. Mr Kelly's son, who was four when he died, asks about his father every day and was now in counselling for anger issues, she explained. She said that both children told their mother they wanted no gifts the Christmas after their father died — they just wanted him back.

As a sign that gardai still have major concerns about the capability of Michael Taylor and his associates, they launched a major operation against the gang in north inner city Dublin just days after his conviction for murder.

More than 150 gardai were involved in the dawn operation on November 24, 2011, which culminated in early morning searches at 17 residential and two business premises as well as six prison cells at Mountjoy Jail connected to the Taylor faction.

Eleven arrests were made as gardai seized a small quantity of herbal cannabis, a haul of shotgun cartridges, cash, drug distribution equipment, documents detailing drug trafficking information as well as financial transactions, computers and a significant number of mobile phones, including some confiscated in Mountjoy.

CHAPTER 13

Black Widow

There was nothing in the modest, rural upbringings of Catherine Scully and Tom Nevin that would suggest that they would become the most talked about couple in Ireland in the early 2000's. Born in 1941, Tom was the eldest of nine children from Tynagh, Co Galway. Ten years younger than him, Catherine grew up with a sister and a brother in a tiny two-bedroom cottage in Nurney, Co Kildare.

While both came from traditional farming backgrounds – they were very different people. As a young woman Catherine was known for her glamorous dress sense and her acute sense of ambition while Tom was a shy man of very few words. Tom Nevin met first met Catherine Scully in 1970 in the Castle Hotel in Dublin – she was working as a receptionist there but was also planning to launch the Catherine Scully Model Agency and Beauty Grooming School at the time while he worked as a bar manager in his uncle's pub - Freehills in Dolphin's Barn, south Dublin.

Tom and Catherine became close friends but it would be a full four years later before they went on their first date. He had been previously married but had both civil and church annulments – at the time, it was still over 20 years before divorce became legal in Ireland.

The couple – both hardworking and ambitious - hit it off and got married in Rome in January, 1976. Catherine Scully became Catherine Nevin and no-one could have imagined at that stage that 20 years later, she would organise her husband's murder – an evil act that would lead to one of most sensational criminal trials in our legal history.

But already Catherine was displaying some of the devious traits which would earn her the nickname 'The Black Widow.' Years later it emerged that she had posed as a social worker in order to meet and scrutinise Tom's first wife June O'Flanagan from Co Mayo. At this stage, Catherine was travelling to schools providing career guidance advice but soon after their marriage, she set up a 'school for ladies' from their house in Mayfield Road, Rialto. Tom's uncle sold the pub in Dolphin's Barn in 1984 and the couple then took over the Barry House pub in Finglas, north Dublin, on a lease. The couple who never had children did well in the bar in the tough north Dublin suburb and were able to buy a number of properties in Dublin - including a house in Clondalkin and a number of flats in Rialto which they rented out.

In 1986, they bought Jack White's Inn in Co Wicklow for IR£260,000 together and invested substantially in upgrading the kitchens. Like nowadays, Ireland in the mid 1980's was gripped by a terrible economic recession and the money that the Nevins invested in the pub was huge by the standards of the time.

But it was located near the popular holiday spot of Brittas Bay on the busy N11, the main road from Dublin to Rosslare Port in Co Wexford and the husband and wife were able to cash in big time on the lucrative passing trade.

While everything was going well for Tom and Catherine from a financial point of view, there were many strains in their marriage – mostly caused by Catherine.

At her murder trial, 14 years after the couple had bought Jack White's, staff at the pub testified that the marriage was a loveless union and purely a business arrangement. The couple had separate bedrooms, and staff members told the court they argued a lot and didn't show each other any affection. Catherine had embarked on a number of affairs with other men from the mid 1980's onwards and in some cases these sexual encounters happened right 'under the nose' of her humiliated husband Tom.

At her murder trial, Catherine claimed that three years into their marriage she became concerned that her husband was having an affair. He was coming home late. She claimed that Tom told her he was a member of the IRA and it would always be part of his life.

There has never been any proof to back up her claims that Tom was a member of the IRA. And gardai would later rubbish these outlandish claims. But what is not in doubt is that by the late 1980's Catherine had decided that her husband had to die and in fact garda investigations would later reveal that between 1989 and 1991, Catherine made a total of 18 requests to three men to have Tom Nevin murdered.

Why did she take this action? Despite everything she has said to the contrary, Catherine must have had a deep pathological hatred of her husband but greed was also a huge factor in her diabolical and often amateurish plotting.

At the time that Catherine had Tom murdered, she stood to gain from two life insurance policies, with Irish Progressive and Irish Life, worth a total of IR£262,500, as well as the proceeds of the sale of Jack White's, which was ultimately disposed of for a sum in excess of IR£600,000. There were also a number of properties in south inner city Dublin which were worth at least IR£ 300,000 at the time of Tom's death.

His murder would make her an instant millionaire while if the couple had simply divorced, Catherine only stood to make around IR£150,000 from the settlement. It has since emerged that the ever ambitious Catherine had planned to set-up a state of the art truck-stop on the N11 route to Rosslare Europort.

Over the course of almost a decade, the so-called 'Black Widow' did everything in her power to have her husband killed before eventually succeeding in March, 1996. It was the behaviour of a psychopath and ultimately the reason why Catherine Nevin was given a life sentence in the Dochas Centre women's prison.

The detailed garda investigation that followed her husband's murder, established that she had attempted to solicit at least three men with alleged connections to the criminal underworld to murder Tom in the years before he was shot dead. All three gave evidence against her. One of these men was convicted fraudster William McClean from Ballinode, Co Monaghan who had a sexual affair with Catherine Nevin in the mid 1980's. This affair ended in the autumn of 1986 and McClean's next contact with the 'Black Widow' was in 1990 when he said that she told him she wanted a "job done" on her husband, and that they weren't getting on.

She mentioned paying around IR£20,000, he claimed. When he asked her why she wanted her husband killed, he said that she replied: "I'd get the insurance money, the lot, everything." McClean later told gardai and then the Central Criminal Court that he told her "no f**king way" and walked out of the room.

Another man that Nevin approached to kill her husband was former IRA man Gerard Heapes who she first met at a Sinn Féin office in Finglas, north Dublin, in 1985. Heapes – a convicted armed robber and alleged garda informer - later revealed that she approached him on at least 10 occasions about killing her husband, and that he went on hearing her crazed propositions because he was curious and intrigued by the whole thing. He had not seen Catherine Nevin for several years when she called out of the blue to his local pub in Finglas around 1990, claiming to have been beaten up by Tom Nevin. "Then she came and dropped the bombshell. She wanted to know would I kill her husband," he explained.

Heapes from St Margaret's, north Dublin, said that she asked him 10 or 12 times to murder her husband. He had told her that a bullet could pass through and hit her. "But she said 'it would look great if Tom died in my arms.'"

Heapes also acknowledged that at one stage he went to Jack White's Inn with a criminal colleague to try to con money out of Nevin over her proposition to shoot her husband. He felt he would get money from her because she wouldn't be able to go to the gardai. Another man that Catherine approached to murder her husband was John Jones, a Finglas-based TV salesman who was running a Sinn Féin advice clinic from the bottom floor of his premises during the 1980s.

Jones revealed he first came across Nevin in 1985 when she came to the advice centre and inquired about buying a pub in the area.

He pointed out that she later leased the Barry House pub with her husband, and they allowed Sinn Féin members to fundraise and sell copies of An Phoblacht in the bar.

He said he was first solicited by Nevin to kill her husband in 1989. He said she told him: "I have a proposition for you. I want you to get the IRA to shoot Tom." Jones from Balbriggan, Co Dublin, said she asked him to get the IRA to murder her husband and make the killing look like a botched hold-up on at least five or six occasions over the course of the next year.

He recalled Catherine had said: "I want you to get the IRA to shoot Tom". Jones "just laughed it off" at first. He finally told her: "I don't want to hear the subject ever again". He claimed that he told her that Sinn Fein was not into that type of thing and reported the approach to more senior members of the organisation.

While Catherine hunted for a contract killer to whack her husband, she continued to court high society including a judge and senior gardai while running Jack White's. Former staff at Jack White's Inn described Catherine as a dedicated social climber and name-dropper. At the pub, those whose professional status impressed Catherine were treated to her free meals and her infamous "special coffees" heavily laced with spirits. But she had a reputation of being mean and unfair to staff at the pub and was known to "scream and roar" at them in public.

She was obsessed with her appearance – was always seen in designer clothes and expensive jewellery. And she even had three cosmetic surgery operations in the late 1980's and early 1990's at Dublin's Mater Private Hospital - liposuction, a tummy tuck, and surgery on her eyelids.

At her murder trial in 2000, sensational allegations of affairs that Nevin was allegedly involved in with a senior district court judge and garda inspector emerged. In the case of Garda Inspector Tom Kennedy it was alleged by a waitress at Jack White' s Inn - Caroline Strahan - that she had seen Kennedy in bed with Catherine "a few times" from 1991 onwards. This was completely denied by the garda.

In his statement to gardai, Tom Kennedy described himself as a friend of Tom Nevin. He said he knew Tom for a number of years, and that this was his reason for going to Jack White's. Mr Kennedy's retirement party had been held at the pub in 1994. He described Catherine Nevin as the type of person who would "give you a pain in the head when she started getting on about things". He said that he was aware of stories going around that he was having a sexual relationship with Catherine, but that this was not true. He said he was over 60 years of age and that sex would not be a concern of his. "I am not into that," he added. "I value my family and my marriage."

Nevin also denied having an affair with the former senior garda when she was questioned about by gardai and again it in the witness box at the Central Criminal Court. But she accepted that she had met him a number of times away from Jack White's, but denied that they had stayed at a hotel in, Ballinaboola, Co Wexford together.

While Inspector Kennedy described himself as a friend of Tom Nevin's and a regular in his pub – these factors led to resentment among other gardai in the area. This is because since moving to the area in 1986, Catherine had made a number of false allegations against other local gardai including that in August 1991 a garda indecently assaulted a 17-year-old barmaid who was working in the pub as well as a false claim that a garda had demanded money with menaces from her. And four gardai gave evidence that they regularly spotted Mr Kennedy's silver-coloured Renault car parked outside the pub during the night.

During the detailed investigation, it emerged that former garda inspector Kennedy was the man who introduced Judge Donnchadh O Buachalla to Catherine Nevin. Judge O'Buachalla denied he had an 'irregular sexual relationship' with Catherine. He also denied having a key to Jack White's pub. Two former bar workers both gave evidence stating that he did have a key. In his statement to gardai, Judge O Buachalla – who is still a serving judge in Co Wexford- said: "I had an excellent relationship with both the late Tom and his wife Catherine. They were both very hospitable. I never stayed overnight and I never had any occasion to have a key to any part of the premises," the judge added.

Like in Tom Kennedy's case, Catherine Nevin also denied ever having an affair with the judge. In December 2000 – eight months after Catherine Nevin was convicted of murdering her husband Tom – a public inquiry found that Judge O' Buachalla made errors of judgement concerning his handling of the licensing of Catherine Nevin's pub – a year after Tom was murdered.

Meanwhile back to the months before Tom was so savagely murdered and it later emerged that the publican was concerned that his wife was trying to have him killed. Tom confided to his step-aunt Patricia Flood around Christmas 1994 that Catherine had demanded that he sell her his share of their pub or else she would, in her words, have him "blown away". His step-aunt told him to leave Catherine and call in the Gardai. "Tom indicated it was not that simple. He said he felt he had no way out," Ms Flood said in her statement to gardai. "She seemed to have a hold over him. He seemed to be a man who didn't care," Ms Flood told officers after Tom's death.

Just over two years later in the early hours of March 19th 1996, Tom Nevin's life was to come to a violent end. He was 54 years of age. The date of the murder was hugely significant – being just after a busy Bank Holiday St Patrick's Day weekend, there would have been lots of cash in Jack White's pub. It seemed like the perfect night to stage a botched robbery or at least that is what Catherine Nevin might have thought.

Gardai received a call - via a panic alarm downstairs in the pub -to go to Jack White's at 4.35 am and arrived at the pub ten minutes later. Detectives Martin MacAndrew and Paul Comiskey arrived at the scene where they discovered the door open and Catherine Nevin lying "slumped on the floor" behind the door and her wrists were tied very tightly behind her back.

The 'Black Widow' was dressed in just a purple silky shirt and white panties. She was gagged with a stocking and her own panties. Her first words to the officers were: "He came into the bedroom. He had a knife. He had a knife and a hood over his head."

Within seconds, gardai discovered the lifeless body of her husband Tom on the kitchen floor – he had been shot through the heart. He had been killed with a single shot from a nine-pellet shotgun fired from close range in the kitchen some time around

3am on March 19 1997.

Meanwhile officers found all the windows and doors secure apart from the front entrance. They discovered Catherine's jewellery box on the hall floor along with items of jewellery scattered around it. When gardai attempted to lift a shocked and pale looking Catherine, she winced, as though with pain. And as she lay on the couch she whispered: "Where's Tom?" The area was now full of gardai as Catherine lay on the couch with her eyes rolling in her head.

She later told officers: "I was awakened by someone pressing my face into the pillow. There was a light coming from the hall as the bedroom light was off. It was a man shouting: 'f**king jewellery, f**king kill ya'. He had a knife in his left hand. Everything in the room was coming down around."

Catherine said she was then tied up by her attacker. She managed to get to a panic button and then the Gardai arrived. Tom was slumped on the kitchen floor in a small pool of blood.

In their first review of the case, officers wondered why she had used a panic button to contact them rather than her mobile phone which was discovered in her bedroom. They also considered why Catherine had not gone into the kitchen to check on the welfare of her husband before they arrived. Some IR£13,000 was taken from the pub that night and the Nevins' car was later found abandoned in Dublin – over an hour's drive up the road.

Gardai at first thought it was a botched robbery and a huge murder investigation kicked off. In a later interview with officers Catherine Nevin described the raiders as "the animals that killed Tom". But her behaviour at this early stage of the investigation was starting to raise alarm bells. At one stage, Nevin refused to give a full statement to gardai, saying she did not trust the local station or Superintendent Pat Flynn. However she later gave a formal statement to the investigation team on the advice of her solicitor where she described her husband as an alcoholic.

Catherine Nevin was also "disruptive and agitated" when a garda fingerprints experts examined her home for prints, two days after Tom was murdered. Almost exactly four years later at the Central Criminal Court, Nevin told a jury that that when she saw her husband's body in Wicklow hospital the night after his murder, she wished she was dead as well. She said there was "no way" she had arranged the killing. And she said she was "absolutely terrified" after being tied up by the armed raiders who shot her husband. She could not remember how she got downstairs from the bedroom where they left her bound and gagged.

This backed up what she had told an increasingly sceptical garda investigation team in the days after the murder. However a few loose ends at the scene of the murder ensured that detectives became very dubious of Nevin's story and led to the Black Widow's downfall.

Firstly, gardai found no signs of forced entry and no evidence of serious ransacking consistent with a frenzied raid that led to murder.

Secondly, only Catherine Nevin's fingerprints were found on the jewellery box and no jewellery was actually taken in the 'raid.'

Furthermore, some days after the incident, Catherine Nevin told one of her sisters-in-law that her ankles had been tied together and then pulled up towards her back and bound to her wrists with her own nylons. But no such ties were ever found.

On the day of Tom Nevin's funeral, Catherine Nevin told Assistant Garda Commissioner Jim McHugh that the smell of the incense at the ceremony reminded her of the gunsmoke she had smelt in the kitchen on the morning of the murder.

But officers realised instantly that it would have been impossible for her to smell the discharge of the shotgun unless she had been in the kitchen shortly after Tom was killed. This conflicted with her statement that she did not go into the kitchen after the raid. Also on the day of the funeral Nevin, who carried a red rose in an act of melodrama as her husband was being buried, wanted to bring guests back to see the bloodstains in the kitchen where Tom was shot.

These factors as well as crucial statements from staff members and people that knew Catherine and Tom very well meant gardai felt they had enough evidence to arrest her in June 1996 – three months after she had organised her husband's murder.

But while being questioned for 48 hours the 'Black Widow' refused to answer any of the questions put to her by the investigation team. This is a tactic which is used more often by terrorists or gangland criminals than by grieving widows and it further increased the garda belief that Nevin was responsible for the murder of her husband. Thirteen months after Tom was murdered, Catherine Nevin was arrested as she collected rent from a property she owned at Ballybough in north inner city Dublin.

She was then charged with the crime as well as soliciting three other people to kill her husband Tom on dates between 1989 and 1990. The three other people were John Jones, Gerry Heapes and William McClean whose highly controversial evidence would be crucial in securing a murder conviction against Catherine Nevin in April 2000.

After her brief appearance before Dublin District Court on April 14, 1997, the Black Widow got her first taste of jail when she was remanded in custody for a week. It would not be her last. A month before she was charged with murder, Nevin had told the High Court: "I was guilty of nothing to do with my husband's murder. I had nothing whatever to do with it."

She made these indignant comments in a hearing where she was fighting her mother-in-law Nora Nevin for control of her late husband's estate. Nevin was released on bail and it would be almost three years before her murder trial kicked off at Dublin's Central Criminal Court before the now deceased judge Miss Justice Mella Carroll.

From the start, the case attracted the sort of media attention which made it legendary and it was engulfed in high drama from word-go. In January 2000, after nine days of dramatic evidence, the trial collapsed when it emerged that the jury's deliberations could be overheard in the public gallery. A re-trial was ordered and a new jury was sworn it but was then discharged on the day the trial was due to start on February 8, 2000, when one member of the jury said she had a condition which prevented her from serving.

It was third time lucky for the trial which finally started for real in late February 2000 – a huge media circus surrounded the case and it gripped the nation for weeks. And why wouldn't it?

Allegations of affairs with a senior garda and respected judge, shadowy crime figures, the savage murder of an innocent publican and right in the middle of it all – the Black Widow who seemed to revel in the blanket publicity. It was ultimately a tale of greed and lust, lies and power – a story that has made Catherine Nevin a household name across Ireland. The trial judge was so concerned about publicity that she banned newspapers from commenting on or publishing photos of Nevin during the trial.

Ms Justice Carroll was outraged about "colour pieces" in newspapers that commented on Nevin's clothing, hairstyle, fingernails and choice of reading material. This included poetry by Kipling and Yeats as well as Seamus Heaney's Booker Prize-winning Translations of Beowulf. And after almost a month of dramatic evidence, the trial almost collapsed again when Nevin was taken ill before she had finished given evidence to the court. The trial was held up for a number of days while she received treatment at St James' Hospital for a mystery sickness. Many people believed it was one last ploy to try and get sympathy from the jury a tactic that didn't work

Looking back on the case, journalist Mary Wilson - who was RTE's highly respected legal affairs correspondent for a decade-described the case as the "most sensational trial that we've had in the last couple of decades."

"You often got the impression as the case was evolving that nobody knew what was going to happen, particularly when she decided to give evidence. In the middle of it all, she disappeared and she's apparently had some type of episode or overdose and she ended up in St James's Hospital overnight and she was back in court again to explain what happened."

Recalling evidence from State witnesses, she said: "There were these characters coming in telling us that she'd actually gone to them and asked them if they'd knock her husband off.

"These weren't trained killers in any sense. There were guys with peripheral links to criminality in some cases and she was going after them to carry out these murders. You had a judge [as a witness], you had a superintendent it was a dream cast for a movie and it was all there. And then you had a jury that went off for about five days to deliberate."

And on Tuesday, April, 11, 2000, when the jury came back after the longest deliberation in the history of the State, they found her guilty of all the charges – that evening there was barely a household in Ireland in which the case was not discussed.

Handing down a mandatory life sentence, Miss Justice Mella Carroll addressed Nevin; she told her she had her husband assassinated and then had tried to have his character assassinated. Nevin stood and looked calmly at the judge as sentence was passed. An emotional Miss Justice Carroll, who presided at the trial for 61 days, through three juries, said that she hoped Tom Nevin's family would take some consolation in this verdict.

The actual hitman who shot Ton Nevin has never been brought to justice and despite much speculation, gardai don't think that Patrick 'Dutchy' Holland – the now deceased gangster who is suspected of murdering crime reporter Veronica Guerin – was the person who killed Tom, three months before Guerin was murdered. 'Dutchy' who died in an English jail in June 2009 had lived in Brittas Bay – close to the pub at the time of Tom Nevin's murder.

Nevin has been locked up since her murder conviction but she has done everything in her power to get out of prison over the past decade. Her first appeal against her murder appeal was dismissed by the courts in 2003.

At the Court of Criminal Appeal in July, 2010, her lawyers won access to Garda files which they claim discredit the evidence of two key prosecution witnesses at her murder trial. Some legal sources have always believed that the case against her is "tainted in the extreme" and at the time of going to press she was currently in the process of launching her third appeal against her murder conviction.

Meanwhile despite being locked up for so long, the 'Black Widow' continued to make headlines for reasons other than her court appeal.

In October 2009, she was cleared of a criminal charge of possessing a mobile phone in prison. During that episode, it emerged that the 'Black Widow' had been in phone contact with Fine Gael Cllr. Bill Tormey who later said he had a moral obligation as a "humanitarian" to speak to Catherine Nevin in prison when he was asked to read her an article on her conviction.

As Nevin remained banged up in jail, there were a number of

hearings in 2012 in which the High Court was asked to rule if Nevin was entitled to her share of joint assets in view of her conviction for Tom Nevin's murder. Mr Nevin's brother and sister, Patrick Nevin and Margaret Lavelle took out a parallel civil case to prevent Mrs Nevin from laying claim to the assets. Bizarrely at one hearing in August, 2012, her lawyers argued that her conviction was 'inadmissible as evidence' as she tried to claim assets belonging to the dead husband she was found guilty of murdering.

Less than a month after these High Court proceedings it emerged that Nevin was due to be freed in 2013 after she managed to convince a prison parole hearing that she deserved a chance to rebuild her life. She is expected to be on a programme of temporary release before being eventually allowed to live permanently in the community again.

There can be no doubt that we have not heard the last of the 'Black Widow' - not by any stretch.